THE
TEACHER'S WORD BOOK

By EDWARD L. THORNDIKE

Professor of Educational Psychology, Teachers College
Columbia University

Second Edition
January, 1927

PUBLISHED BY
𝕿𝖊𝖆𝖈𝖍𝖊𝖗𝖘 𝕮𝖔𝖑𝖑𝖊𝖌𝖊, 𝕮𝖔𝖑𝖚𝖒𝖇𝖎𝖆 𝖀𝖓𝖎𝖛𝖊𝖗𝖘𝖎𝖙𝖞
NEW YORK CITY
1921

10H.1.27

INSTRUCTIONS FOR USING THE TEACHER'S WORD BOOK

THE TEACHER'S WORD BOOK is an alphabetical list of the 10,000 words which are found to occur most widely in a count of about 625,000 words from literature for children; about 3,000,000 words from the Bible and English classics; about 300,000 words from elementary-school text books; about 50,000 words from books about cooking, sewing, farming, the trades, and the like; about 90,000 words from the daily newspapers; and about 500,-000 words from correspondence. Forty-one different sources were used.

A measure of the range and frequency of each word's occurrence is given by the credit-number following it. *Range* answers the question, "How many of these forty-one different sources use the word?" or "How *widely* is the word used?" *Frequency* answers the question, "How *often* is the word used?" If this credit-number is 49 or over, it means that the word is in the 1st 1000 for importance. A credit-number from 29 to 48 means that the word is in the 2nd 1000. A credit of 19 to 28 places it in the 3rd 1000. A credit of 14 to 18 places it in the 4th 1000. A credit of 10 to 13 places it in the 5th 1000 (reaching to 5144 to be exact). The other 5000 words are those with credit of 9 (400 words); 8 (503 words); 7 (571 words); 6 (644 words); 5 (883 words); 4 (1045 words); and 3 (810 words).

In the case of the 5000 most important words, the credit number is followed by a number and letter stating in which thousand and in which half thereof the word belongs. Thus "43 2a" means that the word has an importance of 43 and is in the 1st half of the 2nd 1000. "21 3b" means that the word has an importance of 21 and is in the 2nd half of the 3rd 1000.

Within the 1st 500 words there is a further distinction into hundreds, 1a1 meaning that the word is one of the 1st 100; 1a2 meaning that it is in the 2nd 100; 1a3 meaning that it is in the 3rd 100, and so on.

This list is not a perfect measure of the importance of words, for two reasons. First, a word may be very important for a pupil or graduate to know and yet not figure largely in the world's reading. Second, tens of thousands of hours of further counting would be required to measure the frequency of occurrence of all of these words with exactness. If a complete count were made, there would probably be several hundred words found more deserving of a place in the top ten thousand than some of those now included, and the order of the list would be somewhat changed.

For certain reasons the credits for abbreviations like *in.*, *bbl.*, *yd.*, *etc.*, are probably too low, and far less reliable than those for words. The concordances, vocabularies, and most of the counts made by others have not paid due attention to abbreviations. However, the list as it stands is far better than any that has hitherto been available and will be a help to all teachers in estimating the commonness and importance of words.

The conscientious and thoughtful teacher now spends much time and thought in deciding what pedagogical treatment to use in the case of the words that offer difficulty to pupils. If she is teaching reading she finds, according to Miller, over nine thousand words[1] used in standard Third Readers. Many of these probably should not be taught at all in that grade; others should be explained at the time to serve the purpose of the story but then left to their fate; others should be thoroughly taught and reviewed. This Word Book helps the teacher to decide quickly which treatment is appropriate by telling her just how important any word is. In teaching history or geography or elementary science, almost any book lesson contains one or more words with which some of the pupils will not be familiar. Which are these, and in which cases should the occasion be used to master the word for future use? Decision obviously depends upon how important the word is. In many cases knowledge of how important the word is is all that is needed for decision.

A second practical service of the Word Book is to provide the less experienced teacher with that knowledge both of the importance of words and of their difficulty which the expert teacher has acquired by years of experience with pupils and with books. The beginner at teaching may profitably take the words in any lesson and try to judge how important each is, checking her estimates by the facts of the Word Book. She can thus obtain by a few hours of easy study what would have required

[1] This number includes, however, many derived forms.

months of difficult learning by class-room experimentation; and the experiences of the class-room will be made much more instructive to her.

A third service to all teachers, from the most expert to those just beginning their training, is to provide a convenient place to record any useful facts about these words by which teaching can be guided and improved. For example, the teacher may jot down after a certain word "5," meaning that she seeks to secure mastery of that word in grade 5; "g 49" meaning that the strategic time and place to teach the word is in connection with the geography work on page 49 of a certain book or syllabus; "ex. by . . ." to remind her of the devices she has found most serviceable to explain the meaning of the word. The Word Book will thus become a real treasure-house of help in a form readily available.

The teacher may also wisely enter in the list words that are of local importance, such as, for New York City, *subway* and *elevated*.

It should be noted that, except for special reasons, separate entries are not made of plurals in *s;* plurals where *y* is replaced by *ies;* adverbs formed by adding *ly;* comparatives and superlatives formed by adding *er* and *est,*[2] or *r* and *st;* verb forms in *s, d, ed*[3] and *ing;* past participles formed by adding *n*, and adjectives formed by adding *n* to proper nouns. For example:

boys, girls, berries	are counted in with *boy, girl, berry*
badly, sadly	are counted in with *bad, sad*
longer, bravest	are counted in with *long, brave*
plays, playing, played	are counted in with *play*
thrown, outgrown	are counted in with *throw, outgrow*
Austrian, Bavarian	are counted in with *Austria, Bavaria*

By entering such derivatives under their primary forms, the list is made shorter and easier to use.

Where separate entries do occur, it is because the derived word is likely to offer some difficulty to pupils, and not to be known easily from knowledge of the primary word. Thus *likely* would not be known from *like; being* and *building* should probably often be learned independently of *be* and *build;* and *coming* may appear in the work of Grade 1 before there has been enough experience of *ing* to enable the pupil to derive it by himself.

---

[2] Including changes of *y* to *ies* and *iest*.

[3] Including changes of *y* to *ies* and *ied*.

It should be noted further that this is *not* a spelling list. If it is used as an aid in the construction of spelling lists, some of the derived forms in *s, ies, ly, er, r, est, st, s, ed, d, ing,* and *n* should be inserted. They may offer notable difficulty in spelling even when easily read and understood by derivation.

A full account of the methods by which this list was selected, of the reliability of the credits attached to the words, and of the uses to which the list may be put, will be found in an article of thirty-seven pages, entitled "Word Knowledge in the Elementary School," by E. L. Thorndike, published in the TEACHERS COLLEGE RECORD for September, 1921.

For convenience in certain uses, there is added on pages 127–134 a list of the 2500 words of most wide and frequent occurrence, arranged in five sets of 500 each.

KEY

In the list of words on pages 1 to 126, the numbers in the first column immediately following the column of words are the credit-numbers. Words having a credit-number of 49 or over are found in the 1st 1000 words in importance; those having a credit-number of 29 to 48 are found in the 2nd 1000, and so on, while those having a credit-number of 8 lie between the 5545th and the 6047th word in importance, and so on. A summary of the scheme follows.

CREDIT–NUMBER	POSITION OF WORD
49 or over	1 to 1000
29 to 48	1001 to 2000
19 to 28	2001 to 3000
14 to 18	3001 to 4000
10 to 13	4001 to 5144
9	5145 to 5544
8	5545 to 6047
7	6048 to 6618
6	6619 to 7262
5	7263 to 8145
4	8146 to 9190
3	9191 to 10000

In the case of the 5000 most important words, the credit-number is followed by a second number combined with a letter which indicates in which thousand and in which half thereof the word belongs. Thus 2a means that the word is in the 1st half of the 2nd 1000, 3b means that the word is in the 2nd half of the 3rd 1000. Within the 1st 500 words there is a further distinction into hundreds, 1a1 meaning that the word is one of the 1st 100; 1a2 meaning that it is in the 2nd 100; 1a3, that it is in the 3rd 100; 1a4, that it is in the 4th 100; 1a5, that it is in the 5th 100.

NOTE.—In the 1927 edition, new words have been added to pp. 12, 13, 20, 47, 51, 58, 60, 66, 68, 71, 74, 84, 110, 121.

A to Acre

a	208	1a1	abuse	21	3b
Aaron	6		abyss	9	
abandon	17	4a	academy	9	
abash(ed)	4		accent	14	4b
abate	10	5b	accept	47	2a
abbey	9		acceptance	9	
abbot	7		access	11	5b
abdomen	5		accessory	4	
Abe	3		accident	26	4a
abed	5		accidental	5	
Abel	5		accommodate	10	5b
abhor	14	4b	accommodation	8	
abide	18	4a	accompaniment	3	
ability	16	4a	accompany	34	2b
abject	7		accomplish	31	2b
able	70	1b	accomplishment	5	
aboard	15	4b	accord	16	4a
abode	17	4a	accordance	8	
abolish	10	5b	according	48	2a
abominable	9		accordingly	20	3b
abomination	5		accost	5	
abound	10	5b	account	63	1b
about	172	1a1	accumulate	3	
above	101	1a3	accurate	3	
Abraham	14	4b	accursed	13	5a
abridge	4		accusation	8	
abroad	23	3a	accuse	22	3b
abrupt	7		accuser	5	
absence	22	3b	accustom	26	3a
absent	25	3a	ache	21	3b
absolute	29	2b	achieve	14	4b
absolve	8		achievement	7	
absorb	8		acid	9	
absorbent	3		acknowledge	18	4a
abstain	6		acorn	10	5b
abstinence	3		acquaint	22	3b
abstract	3		acquaintance	26	3a
absurd	8		acquire	20	3b
abundance	21	3b	acquit	3	
abundant	21	3b	acre	34	2b

across	84	1a5	adopt	23	3a
act	70	1b	adoption	10	5b
action	36	2a	adoration	3	
active	24	3a	adore	16	4a
activity	7		adorn	17	4a
actor	13	5a	adornment	3	
actress	3		adult	5	
actual	31	2b	adultery	4	
acute	5		advance	45	2a
Adam	13	5a	advancement	8	
Adams	4		advantage	40	2a
adapt	5		advantageous	3	
add	75	1a	adventure	22	3b
addition	28	2b	adventurer	4	
additional	11	5b	adventurous	7	
address	45	2a	adverb	4	
adequate	3		adversary	10	5b
adhere	3		adverse	8	
adieu	8		adversity	7	
adjacent	6		advertise	12	5a
adjective	6		advertisement	7	
adjoin	12	5a	advice	30	2b
adjourn	3		advisable	3	
adjudge	4		advise	29	2b
adjust	9		adviser	5	
adjustment	5		advocate	5	
administer	6		adze	4	
administration	12	5a	Aeneas	4	
administrator	5		aerial	5	
admirable	6		aeroplane	4	
admiral	12	5a	afar	11	5b
admiration	16	4a	affair	34	2b
admire	36	2a	affect	27	3a
admirer	6		affection	21	3b
admission	10	5b	affectionate	10	5b
admit	33	2b	affirm	13	5a
admittance	4		afflict	13	5a
admonish	9		affliction	11	5b
admonition	4		afford	23	3a
ado	6		affright(ed)	12	5a

allow	63	1b		ambition	23	3a
allowable	4			ambitious	15	4b
allowance	6			ambush	6	
allure	11	5b		amen	8	
ally	5			amend	12	5a
almanac	5			amendment	16	4a
almighty	13	5a		America	48	2a
almond	7			American	56	1b
almost	90	1a4		amiable	8	
alms	13	5a		amid	13	5a
aloes	4			amidst	4	
aloft	10	5b		amiss	8	
alone	89	1a4		amity	4	
along	99	1a3		ammonia	5	
alongside	5			ammunition	7	
aloof	9			among	106	1a3
aloud	26	3a		amongst	8	
alphabet	5			amount	51	1b
Alps	9			ample	20	3b
already	73	1b		Amsterdam	7	
also	119	1a2		amuse	17	4a
altar	22	3b		amusement	10	5b
alter	21	3b		Amy	6	
alteration	5			an	181	1a1
alternate	8			analysis	5	
although	68	1b		anarchy	4	
altitude	8			ancestor	16	4a
altogether	21	3b		anchor	21	3b
aluminum	3			ancient	37	2a
alumni	4			and	210	1a1
always	94	1a4		Anderson	4	
am	91	1a4		Andes	5	
amain	7			Andrew	14	4b
amateur	4			anecdote	5	
amaze	19	3b		anew	7	
amazement	11	5b		angel	40	2a
Amazon	7			angelic	6	
ambassador	13	5a		anger	36	2a
amber	11	5b		angle	15	4b
ambiguous	3			angrily	3	

angry	47	2a		any	158	1a1
anguish	11	5b		anybody	21	3b
animal	70	1b		anyhow	9	
animate	8			anyone	20	3b
animosity	3			anything	58	1b
ankle	16	4a		anyway	14	4b
Ann	7			anywhere	15	4b
Anna	12	5a		apace	5	
annal	5			apart	39	2a
Anne	14	4b		apartment	12	5a
annex	5			ape	9	
Annie	6			aperture	6	
annihilate	3			apiece	12	5a
anniversary	10	5b		Apollo	6	
announce	10	5b		apology	4	
announcement	7			apostle	4	
annoy	10	5b		apothecary	4	
annoyance	4			Appalachian	4	
annual	26	3a		appall	6	
anoint	10	5b		apparatus	7	
anon	11	5b		apparel	10	5b
another	116	1a2		apparent	15	4b
answer	91	1a4		apparition	6	
ant	16	4a		appeal	25	3a
antagonist	3			appear	70	1b
antarctic	4			appearance	32	2b
Anthony	5			appease	9	
anthracite	3			appertain	4	
anti	5			appetite	21	3b
antic	4			applaud	8	
anticipate	7			applause	13	5a
Antioch	5			apple	78	1a5
antique	8			appliance	4	
antiquity	10	5b		applicant	5	
antiseptic	3			application	21	3b
Antonio	4			applied (*see* apply)		
Antony	4			apply	36	2a
anvil	10	5b		appoint	38	2a
anxiety	5			appointment	15	4b
anxious	29	2b		appreciate	13	5a

appreciation	4		aristocratic	7	
appreciative	3		arithmetic	6	
apprehend	8		Arizona	5	
apprehension	6		ark	12	5a
apprehensive	3		Arkansas	5	
approach	43	2a	arm	96	1a3
approbation	4		armful	3	
appropriate	6		armhole	5	
approval	6		armor(ed)	27	3a
approve	30	2b	army	59	1b
approximate	4		arose	27	3a
apricot	4		around	95	1a3
April	39	2a	arouse	11	5b
apron	22	3b	arrange	35	2b
apt	12	5a	arrangement	13	5a
aquarium	4		arrant	7	
Arab	8		array	16	4a
Arabia(n)	14	4b	arrest	18	4a
Aragon	4		arrival	21	3b
arbitrary	5		arrive	57	1b
arbor	9		arrogant	5	
arch	29	2b	arrow	29	2b
archbishop	6		arsenal	4	
archer	6		art	68	1b
architect	5		artful	6	
architecture	6		Arthur	19	3b
archway	4		article	52	1b
arctic	11	5b	artificial	12	5a
ardent	6		artillery	6	
ardor	5		artisan	4	
are	183	1a1	artist	21	3b
area	25	3a	artistic	11	5b
aren't	6		artless	4	
Argentina (e)	8		as	204	1a1
argue	11	5b	ascend	24	3a
argument	19	3b	ascent	5	
Ariel	5		ascertain	7	
aright	4		ascribe	7	
arise	24	3a	ash (ashes)	23	3a
(*see also* arose)			ashamed	29	2b

ashore	16	4a		astronomy	3	
Asia	28	2b		asunder	10	5b
aside	27	3a		asylum	3	
ask	94	1a4		at	203	1a1
asleep	48	2a		ate	33	2b
asparagus	6			Athenian	7	
aspect	10	5b		Athens	10	5b
asphalt	5			athletic	11	5b
aspiration	6			athwart	4	
aspire	8			Atlanta	3	
ass	21	3b		Atlantic	35	2b
assail	11	5b		atmosphere	11	5b
assassinate	3			atom	4	
assault	15	4b		atone	4	
assay	6			atonement	4	
assemblage	4			attach	20	3b
assemble	23	3a		attachment	5	
assembly	25	3a		attack	33	2b
assent	6			attain	21	3b
assert	14	4b		attainment	3	
assess	4			attempt	38	2a
assessment	3			attend	57	1b
assign	20	3b		attendance	12	5a
assignment	4			attendant	13	5a
assist	29	2b		attention	35	2b
assistance	17	4a		attentive	13	5a
assistant	8			attest	8	
associate	21	3b		attic	10	5b
association	15	4b		attire	14	4b
assortment	5			attitude	10	5b
assume	20	3b		attorney	13	5a
assurance	11	5b		attract	17	4a
assure	34	2b		attraction	10	5b
assuredly	3			attractive	16	4a
Assyria(n)	6			attribute	10	5b
aster	3			auburn	6	
astonish	23	3a		auction	4	
astonishment	11	5b		auctioneer	3	
astound	4			audacious	3	
astray	6			audible	5	

audience	16	4a		away	125	1a2
Aug.	9			awe	17	4a
auger	4			awful	33	2b
aught	8			awhile	20	3b
augment	7			awkward	9	
August	37	2a		awning	4	
Augustus	5			awoke	13	5a
aunt	40	2a		ax (axe)	30	2b
aurora	4			axis	8	
austere	6			axle	8	
Australia(n)	12	5a		Axminster	4	
Austria(n)	11	5b		ay	12	5a
authentic	6			aye	7	
author	27	3a		azure	8	
authority	28	2b				
authorize	7			baa	5	
auto	13	5a		babble	14	4b
automatic	7			babbler	4	
automobile	33	2b		babe	17	4a
autumn	35	2b		(*see* baby *and* babies)		
autumnal	4			Babel	4	
auxiliary	4			baby (ies)	61	1b
avail	11	5b		Babylon	9	
available	5			bachelor	8	
avalanche	3			back	133	1a2
avarice	8			backbone	5	
Ave.	3			backward	22	3b
avenge	11	5b		bacon	18	4a
avenger	4			bad	82	1a5
avenue	30	2b		bade	26	3a
average	24	3a		badge	9	
aversion	4			badger	7	
avert	4			baffle	7	
avoid	31	2b		bag	57	1b
await	32	2b		baggage	7	
awake	41	2a		bagpipe	5	
(*see* awoke)				bail	6	
awaken	14	4b		bait	13	5a
award	7			bake	41	2a
aware	11	5b		baker	18	4a

balance	31	2b	bargain	23	3a
balcony	4		barge	8	
bald	9		bark	48	2a
bale	5		barley	18	4a
balk	4		barn	41	2a
ball	76	1a5	barnyard	7	
ballad	8		baron	10	5b
balloon	5		barrel	25	3a
ballot	6		barren	19	3b
balm	13	5a	barrette	4	
balmy	7		barrier	11	5b
Baltic	4		barrow	4	
Baltimore	14	4b	barter	3	
bamboo	8		base	48	2a
ban	4		baseball	10	5b
banana	14	4b	basement	4	
band	57	1b	baseness	5	
bandage	5		bashful	11	5b
bandit	4		bashfulness	3	
bang	10	5b	basin	20	3b
banish	19	3b	basis	14	4b
banishment	10	5b	bask	4	
banjo	4		basket	54	1b
bank	83	1a5	bass	7	
banker	10	5b	bastard	8	
bankrupt	4		baste	5	
bankruptcy	3		bastings	3	
banner	22	3b	bat	19	3b
bannock	6		bath	27	3a
banquet	21	3b	bathe	27	3a
baptism	7		bathrobe	3	
Baptist	6		bathroom	6	
baptize	6		batiste	4	
bar	44	2a	battalion	3	
barbarian	7		batter	7	
barbarous	11	5b	battery	12	5a
barber	12	5a	battle	57	1b
bard	12	5a	battlement	5	
bare	47	2a	battleship	4	
barefoot	8		bauble	5	

bawl	6		beech	8	
bay	52	1b	beef	20	3b
bayonet	7		been	159	1a1
bbl. (bbls.)	4		beer	12	5a
be	206	1a1	beet	11	5b
beach	30	2b	beetle	11	5b
beacon	5		befall	16	4a
bead	22	3b	befell	5	
beading	4		before	159	1a1
beak	12	5a	beforehand	10	5b
beam	44	2a	befriend	6	
bean	30	2b	beg	45	2a
beanstock	6		began	73	1b
bear	92	1a4	beget	9	
beard	29	2b	beggar	24	3a
bearer	10	5b	beggarly	3	
bearing (*noun*)	6		begin	97	1a3
beast	56	1b	beginner	6	
beat	69	1b	begone	4	
beaten	8		begot	8	
beau	9		beguile	13	5a
beauteous	9		begun	35	2b
beautiful	75	1a	behalf	16	4a
beautify	6		behave	16	4a
beauty	55	1b	behavior	7	
beaver	8		behead	8	
became	48	2a	beheld	22	3b
because	108	1a3	behind	95	1a3
beck	4		behold	37	2a
beckon	10	5b	being	91	1a4
become	88	1a4	belated	4	
bed	105	1a3	belch	4	
bedchamber	3		belfry	3	
bedding	4		Belgian	4	
bedlam	4		Belgium	8	
bedroom	17	4a	belie	4	
bedspread	4		belief	19	3b
bedstead	4		believe	77	1a5
bedtime	6		believer	5	
bee	58	1b	bell	66	1b

belle	4		betake	4	
bellow	16	4a	Beth	6	
belly	10	5b	bethink	6	
belong	62	1b	Bethlehem	6	
beloved	19	3b	bethought	4	
below	46	2a	betide	5	
belt	31	2b	betimes	6	
bemoan	4		betray	23	3a
Ben	9		betroth(ed)	9	
bench	33	2b	better	105	1a3
bend	40	2a	Betty	18	4a
beneath	39	2a	between	119	1a2
benediction	4		betwixt	8	
benefactor	4		bevel	5	
benefit	30	2b	bewail	10	5b
benevolence	4		beware	14	4b
benign	5		bewilder(ed)	5	
Benjamin	13	5a	bewitch	8	
bent	29	2b	beyond	29	2b
benzine	3		bias	8	
bequeath	6		bib	7	
bereave	6		bible	14	4b
bereft	7		bicycle	16	4a
Berkeley	7		bid	42	2a
Berlin	6		bide	9	
berry	31	2b	bier	6	
berth	5		big (ger, gest)	89	1a4
beseech	11	5b	bill (B)	67	1b
beseem	6		billow	12	5a
beset	9		Billy	23	3a
beside	58	1b	bin	6	
besides	13	5a	bind	36	2a
besiege	12	5a	binder	4	
besought	5		biography	3	
bespeak	4		birch	14	4b
Bess	16	4a	bird	79	1a5
best	107	1a3	birdie	9	
bestow	20	3b	birth	37	2a
bestride	4		birthday	34	2b
bet	9		birthplace	7	

birthright	7		blight	7	
biscuit	8		blind	51	1b
bishop	15	4b	blindness	11	5b
bit	50	1b	blink	6	
bite	37	2a	bliss	17	4a
bitter	36	2a	blissful	5	
bitterness	9		blister	9	
black (B)	99	1a3	blithe	7	
blackberry	7		blizzard	4	
blackbird	10	5b	block	47	2a
blackboard	16	4a	blockhead	3	
blacken	7		blond	6	
blackness	6		blood	57	1b
blacksmith	24	3a	bloody	19	3b
bladder	5		bloom	34	2b
blade	30	2b	bloomer(s)	4	
blame	41	2a	blossom	38	2a
blameless	9		blot	18	4a
blanch	7		blouse	8	
Blanche	7		blow	84	1a5
bland	5		blue	82	1a5
blank	24	3a	bluebell	4	
blanket	15	4b	bluebird	6	
blaspheme	6		bluefish	4	
blasphemy	8		bluff	12	5a
blast	24	3a	blunder	5	
blaze	28	2b	blunt	14	4b
blazon	5		blur	3	
bleach	9		blush	23	3a
bleak	9		bluster	5	
bleat	12	5a	boar	7	
bled	6		board	71	1b
bleed	18	4a	boarder	4	
blemish	8		boast	35	2b
blend	15	4b	boat	58	1b
bless	52	1b	boatman	3	
blessedness	4		bob (B)	21	3b
blessing	30	2b	Bobby	8	
blest	14	4b	bobolink	6	
blew	27	3a	bode	5	

bodily 9

body	83	1a5	bosom	28	2b
bog	12	5a	boss	8	
Bohemia(n)	6		Boston	19	3b
boil	37	2a	botanical	3	
boiler	8		botany	4	
boisterous	8		both	115	1a2
bold	42	2a	bother	16	4a
boldness	8		bottle	47	2a
bolster	5		bottom	58	1b
bolt	24	3a	bottomless	3	
bomb	4		bough	23	3a
bombard	3		bought	46	2a
bonbon	6		bounce	7	
bond	25	3a	bound	46	2a
bondage	10	5b	boundary	21	3b
bondman	6		boundless	13	5a
bone	59	1b	bounteous	8	
bonfire	3		bountiful	5	
bonnet	17	4a	bounty	13	5a
bonny	5		bouquet	8	
bonus	3		bout	6	
boo	4		bow	59	1b
book	114	1a2	bowel	14	4b
bookcase	6		bower	19	3b
booklet	4		bowl	45	2a
boom	6		box(es)	75	1a
boon	11	5b	boxer	3	
boost	3		boy	122	1a2
boot	31	2b	boyhood	7	
booth	12	5a	boyish	4	
booty	6		brace	13	5a
bo-peep	8		bracelet	12	5a
borax	4		bracket	4	
border	39	2a	brag	6	
bore	35	2b	braid	15	4b
boric	4		brain	27	3a
born	59	1b	brake	23	3a
borne	20	3b	bramble	10	5b
borrow	27	3a	bran	10	5b
borrower	3		branch	63	1b

borough 9

brand	21	3b	bright	74	1b
brandish	6		brighten	15	4b
brass	28	2b	brightness	12	5a
brassiere	5		brilliant	16	4a
brave	55	1b	brim	18	4a
bravery	12	5a	brimstone	6	
brawl	8		brine	5	
brawn	4		bring	110	1a3
bray	5		bringer		
brazen	9		brink	11	5b
Brazil	10	5b	brisk	12	5a
breach	9		bristle	6	
bread	78	1a5	Britain	19	3b
breadth	19	3b	British	30	2b
break	73	1b	Briton	9	
breaker	7		brittle	6	
breakfast	50	1b	broach	5	
breast	44	2a	broad	54	1b
breath	44	2a	broaden	3	
breathe	44	2a	Broadway	8	
breathless	7		broider	4	
bred	17	4a	broil	7	
breeches	9		broke	28	2b
breed(ing)	22	3b	broken	59	1b
breeze	25	3a	broker	3	
breezy	5		bronchitis	3	
Bremen	6		bronze	9	
brethren	18	4a	brooch	5	
brevity	4		brood	17	4a
brew	8		brook	52	1b
briar	18	4a	brooklet	5	
bribe	11	5b	Brooklyn	17	4a
brick	40	2a	broom	21	3b
bridal	10	5b	broth	5	
bride	28	2b	brother	87	1a4
bridegroom	9		brotherhood	8	
bridge	64	1b	brotherly	10	5b
bridle	20	3b	brought	76	1a5
brief	32	2b	brow	28	2b
brigade	4		brown (B)	69	1b

brownie (B)	11	5b		bumble	4	
browse	4			bump	9	
bruin	5			bumper	4	
bruise	18	4a		bun	8	
brush	38	2a		bunch	27	3a
Brussels	6			bundle	22	3b
brutal	8			bunion	3	
brute	15	4b		bunny	4	
brutish	5			bunting	7	
Brutus	5			burden	25	3a
bu.	9			burdensome	4	
bubble	24	3a		bureau	20	3b
buccaneer	4			burgess	6	
buck	4			burgher	6	
bucket	18	4a		burglar	5	
buckle	9			burial	16	4a
buckler	5			buried (see bury)		
buckwheat	9			burn	77	1a5
bud	29	2b		burner	6	
budge	5			burnish	6	
budget	6			burr	11	5b
buff	9			burst	40	2a
buffalo (B)	8			bury	38	2a
buffer	4			bus	6	
buffet	11	5b		bush(es)	45	2a
bug	12	5a		bushel	26	3a
buggy	9			bushing	4	
bugle	14	4b		bushy	3	
build	77	1a5		busily	8	
builder	18	4a		business	73	1b
building	57	1b		bust	12	5a
built	55	1b		bustle	7	
bulb	10	5b		busy	57	1b
bulk	16	4a		but	196	1a1
bull	26	3a		butcher	24	3a
bullet	11	5b		butler	6	
bulletin	6			butt	8	
bullock	5			butter	55	1b
bully	5			buttercup	5	
bulwark	6			butterfly	20	3b

button	28	2b	camera	6	
buy	80	1a5	Camilla	3	
buyer	8		camp	43	2a
buzz	22	3b	campaign	14	4b
by	191	1a1	camper	3	
bye	11	5b	camphor	5	
			can	163	1a1
¢ or c. (*for* cent)	9		Canaan	5	
cab	10	5b	Canaanite	3	
cabbage	15	4b	Canada	21	3b
cabin	20	3b	canal	25	3a
cabinet	15	4b	canary	6	
cable	14	4b	cancel	4	
Cabot	6		candid	3	
cackle	6		candidacy	3	
Caesar	19	3b	candidate	16	4a
café	3		candle	31	2b
cage	21	3b	candlestick	8	
Cain	9		candor	3	
Cairo	3		candy	30	2b
cake	56	1b	cane	21	3b
Calais	7		canker	6	
calamity	10	5b	canned	4	
calculate	5		cannibal	5	
calculation	3		cannon	20	3b
Caleb	3		cannot	70	1b
calendar	11	5b	canoe	14	4b
calf	16	4a	canon	4	
calico	6		canopy	4	
California	24	3a	canst	25	3a
call	146	1a2	can't	33	2b
caller	3		Canterbury	5	
calm	35	2b	canton	5	
calmness	3		canvas	20	3b
calomel	4		canyon	3	
calves	10	5b	cap	53	1b
cambric	6		capable	19	3b
Cambridge	6		capacious	8	
came	113	1a2	capacity	16	4a
camel	15	4b	cape	26	3a

caper	7		carrion	4	
capital	35	2b	carrot	6	
capitol	7		carry	108	1a3
caprice	3		cart	27	3a
capricious	4		carter (C)	7	
captain	56	1b	cartoon	3	
captivate	3		Caruso	4	
captive	18	4a	carve	23	3a
captivity	10	5b	cascade	10	5b
capture	22	3b	cascara	3	
Capulet	3		case	77	1a5
car	52	1b	casement	9	
caramel	6		cash	21	3b
caravan	9		cashier	8	
carbolic	6		cask	7	
carbon	5		casket	5	
carbuncle	3		casque	5	
carburetor	6		casserole	4	
carcass	5		cast	48	2a
card	48	2a	castile (C)	8	
cardboard	4		Castilian	5	
cardinal	9		castle	46	2a
care	98	1a3	castor	4	
career	14	4b	casual	8	
careful	59	1b	casualty	3	
careless	22	3b	cat	46	2a
caress	10	5b	catalogue	10	5b
cargo	14	4b	cataract	9	
Carl	14	4b	catarrh	4	
Carmel	3		catastrophe	5	
carnal	6		catch(es)	69	1b
carnation	3		catcher	4	
carnival	4		caterpillar	8	
carol	7		cathedral	15	4b
Carolina	13	5a	Catherine	5	
carouse	3		Catholic	15	4b
carpenter	24	3a	catnip	3	
carpet	20	3b	Cato	4	
carriage	39	2a	Catskill	4	
carrier	12	5a	cattle	45	2a

caught	47	2a	certify	4	
cauliflower	4		chafe	9	
cause	79	1a5	chaff	12	5a
causeless	3		chain	49	1b
caustic	3		chair	59	1b
caution	8		chairman	11	5b
cautious	8		Chaldea(n)	3	
cavalier	6		chalk	13	5a
cavalry	5		challenge	9	
cave	31	2b	challis (ie)	4	
cavern	8		chamber	38	2a
caw	10	5b	chamberlain	7	
cease	33	2b	chambray	7	
ceaseless	6		chamois	3	
Cecil	3		champaign	8	
cedar	19	3b	champion	17	4a
ceiling	14	4b	Champlain	5	
celebrate	30	2b	chance	55	1b
celebration	10	5b	chancellor	8	
celery	10	5b	chandelier	4	
celestial	15	4b	change	101	1a3
cell	23	3a	changeable	4	
cellar	26	3a	changeful	3	
celluloid	3		channel	22	3b
cement	16	4a	chant	12	5a
cemetery	11	5b	chanticleer	7	
censer	5		chaos	8	
censure	11	5b	chap	7	
census	3		chapel	24	3a
cent	51	1b	chaperon	4	
center	63	1b	chapter	18	4a
central	32	2b	character	44	2a
century	32	2b	characteristic	10	5b
cereal	6		characterize	3	
ceremonial	3		charcoal	6	
ceremony	16	4a	charge	71	1b
Ceres	3		chargeable	4	
certain	77	1a5	charger	7	
certainty	5		chariot	20	3b
certificate	11	5b	charitable	7	

charity	23	3a	chest	29	2b
Charles	40	2a	Chester	5	
Charleston	7		chestnut	22	3b
Charley (ie)	8		cheviot	5	
charm	42	2a	chew	9	
chart	11	5b	Chicago	21	3b
charter	15	4b	chick	20	3b
chase	37	2a	chicken	46	2a
chasm	5		chide	7	
chaste	11	5b	chief	64	1b
chasten	5		chiffon	5	
chastise	6		chiffonnier	5	
chastisement	5		child	85	1a4
chastity	5		childhood	17	4a
chat	11	5b	childish	10	5b
chatter	18	4a	childless	5	
chauffeur	6		childlike	5	
Chautauqua	5		children	88	1a4
cheap	34	2b	Chile	7	
cheat	16	4a	chill	24	3a
check	47	2a	chilly	6	
checkers	7		chime	17	4a
cheek	43	2a	chimney	30	2b
cheer	46	2a	chin	17	4a
cheerful	30	2b	china (C)	29	2b
cheerfulness	4		Chinaman	4	
cheerily	6		Chinese	12	5a
cheerless	3		chink	8	
cheery	10	5b	chip	15	4b
cheese	32	2b	chirp	13	5a
chemical	4		chisel	8	
chemise	6		chivalry	9	
chemistry	3		chocolate	18	4a
cheque	4		choice	37	2a
chequer(ed)	5		choir	15	4b
cherish	12	5a	choke	17	4a
cherry	33	2b	choleric	4	
cherub	8		choose	51	1b
cherubim	7		chop	24	3a
chess	4		chopper	4	

chord	6		civil	24	3a
chorus	6		civility	4	
chose(n)	40	2a	civilization	5	
Christ	19	3b	civilize	9	
christen	3		clad	17	4a
Christendom	5		claim	45	2a
Christian	34	2b	clam	10	5b
Christianity	3		clamber	5	
Christmas	62	1b	clamor	14	4b
Christopher	5		clamorous	5	
chronicle	12	5a	clamp	5	
chrysanthemum	3		clan	4	
chuck	8		clang	10	5b
chuckle	8		clap	26	3a
chum	4		Clara	5	
church	81	1a5	Clarence	7	
churchman	5		Clark	6	
churchyard	9		clash	10	5b
churl	5		clasp	24	3a
churlish	4		class	60	1b
cider	8		classic	14	4b
cigar	11	5b	classify	3	
cigarette	3		classmate	3	
Cincinnati	6		clatter	11	5b
cinder	7		Claus	7	
Cinderella	11	5b	clause	12	5a
cipher	3		claw	12	5a
circle	49	1b	clay	32	2b
circuit	13	5a	clean	67	1b
circular	18	4a	cleaner (*noun*)	6	
circulate	3		cleanse	13	5a
circulation	6		clear	88	1a4
circumference	5		clearness	4	
circumstance	24	3a	cleave	16	4a
circus	13	5a	cleaver	4	
cistern	10	5b	cleft	10	5b
cite	8		clemency	3	
citizen	31	2b	clench	4	
city	114	1a2	Cleopatra	4	
civic	5		clergy	5	

churn 11 5b

clergyman	7		coachman	8	
clerk	35	2b	coal	57	1b
Cleveland	11	5b	coarse	27	3a
clever	16	4a	coast	54	1b
client	6		coat	74	1b
cliff	24	3a	coax	6	
Clifford	9		cob	6	
climate	26	3a	cobbler	12	5a
climb	47	2a	cobweb	6	
clime	13	5a	cock	39	2a
cling	12	5a	cockle	5	
clink	5		cocoa	7	
Clinton	4		coconut	8	
clip	16	4a	cocoon	3	
cloak	30	2b	cod	15	4b
clock	53	1b	code	5	
clod	7		codfish	3	
clog	4		coffee	38	2a
cloister	5		coffer	6	
close	105	1a3	coffin	11	5b
closet	21	3b	cog	3	
cloth	54	1b	coil	10	5b
clothe (ing)	50	1b	coin	35	2b
clothes (*noun*)	68	1b	coincidence	3	
cloud	67	1b	cold	104	1a3
cloudless	4		colic	3	
cloudy	19	3b	collapse	4	
clove	11	5b	collar	33	2b
clover	14	4b	collect	31	2b
clown	7		collection	21	3b
cloy	5		college	45	2a
club	34	2b	collision	4	
cluck	14	4b	cologne (C)	8	
clumsy	6		Colombia(n)	17	4a
clung	8		colonel	7	
Cluny	4		colonial	10	5b
cluster	20	3b	colonist	16	4a
clutch	13	5a	colony	35	2b
co.	3		color	84	1a5
coach	29	2b	Colorado	12	5a

colt	25	3a
Columbia	17	4a
Columbus	24	3a
column	24	3a
comb	17	4a
combat	16	4a
combatant	3	
combination	19	3b
combine	24	3a
come	151	1a1
(*see also* coming)		
comedian	3	
comedy	12	5a
comely	9	
comer(s)	4	
comet	7	
comfort	44	2a
comfortable (ly)	33	2b
comforter	11	5b
comfortless	5	
comical	4	
coming	69	1b
command	57	1b
commander	15	4b
commandment	9	
commence	21	3b
commencement	3	
commend	19	3b
commendation	6	
comment	8	
commerce	34	2b
commercial	22	3b
commission	22	3b
commissioner	14	4b
commit	22	3b
committee	22	3b
commodious	3	
commodity	6	
common	62	1b
commonplace	3	

commonwealth	10	5b
commotion	7	
commune	8	
communicate	9	
communication	15	4b
communion	7	
community	15	4b
compact	13	5a
companion	38	2a
company	78	1a5
comparable	3	
comparative	11	5b
compare	48	2a
comparison	16	4a
compartment	3	
compass	29	2b
compassion	11	5b
compel	27	3a
compensate	3	
compensation	4	
compete	6	
competence	3	
competent	4	
competition	9	
compile	3	
complain	28	2b
complaint	17	4a
complement	7	
complete	51	1b
completion	4	
complexion	10	5b
compliance	3	
complicate	4	
complication	3	
compliment	11	5b
comply	10	5b
compose	18	4a
composition	15	4b
composure	5	
compound	11	5b

comprehend	14	4b		confession	11	5b
compress	4			confessor	6	
comprise	7			confide	5	
compromise	5			confidence	22	3b
compulsion	4			confident	13	5a
comrade	18	4a		confidential	4	
con	4			confine	18	4a
conceal	23	3a		confiner	5	
concealment	3			confirm	18	4a
concede	4			confirmation	9	
conceit	10	5b		conflagration	3	
conceive	20	3b		conflict	14	4b
concentrate	5			conform	5	
conception	7			conformity	5	
concern	31	2b		confound	16	4a
concerning	16	4a		confront	3	
concert	18	4a		confuse	13	5a
concession	3			confusion	19	3b
conclude	27	3a		congenial	5	
conclusion	12	5a		congratulate	10	5b
concord	7			congratulation	6	
concrete	9			congregate	5	
concur	4			congregation	11	5b
condemn	23	3a		congress	28	2b
condemnation	6			congressional	3	
condense	9			conjecture	8	
condescend	4			conjugation	5	
condition	49	1b		conjunction	4	
conditional	3			conjure	6	
conduct	34	2b		connect	37	2a
conductor	12	5a		Connecticut	11	5b
conduit	5			connection	21	3b
cone	10	5b		conquer	33	2b
confectioner	3			conqueror	17	4a
confederacy	8			conquest	19	3b
confederate	7			conscience	24	3a
confederation	4			conscientious	4	
confer	17	4a		conscious	14	4b
conference	14	4b		consciousness	5	
confess	25	3a		consecrate	12	5a

consecration	7	
consent	40	2a
consequence	19	3b
consequent(ly)	13	5a
conserve	5	
consider	46	2a
considerable	17	4a
considerably	6	
consideration	14	4b
consist	33	2b
consistent	4	
consolation	9	
console	5	
consonant	5	
consort	8	
conspicuous	8	
conspiracy	11	5b
conspire	9	
constable	8	
constancy	5	
constant	37	2a
Constantinople	6	
constitute	13	5a
constitution	21	3b
constrain	10	5b
constraint	5	
construct	19	3b
construction	17	4a
consul	9	
consult	22	3b
consultation	7	
consume	16	4a
consumer	3	
consumption	8	
contact	4	
contagion	4	
contagious	5	
contain	56	1b
container	3	
contemplate	8	

contemplation	8	
contemporary	7	
contempt	15	4b
contemptible	5	
contend	17	4a
content	47	2a
contentedly	7	
contention	8	
contentment	5	
contest	21	3b
continent	26	3a
continental	5	
continual	22	3b
continuance	7	
continuation	6	
continue	66	1b
continuous	14	4b
contract	24	3a
contractor	3	
contradict	5	
contradiction	5	
contrary	26	3a
contrast	14	4b
contribute	10	5b
contribution	6	
contrive	9	
control	31	2b
controversy	9	
convene	6	
convenience	12	5a
convenient	23	3a
convent	13	5a
convention	17	4a
conversation	24	3a
converse	13	5a
convert	15	4b
convey	15	4b
convict		
convict		
convince	22	3b

coo	8		cottage	28	2b
cook	57	1b	cotton	39	2a
cooky	7		couch	24	3a
cool	61	1b	cough	16	4a
cooler (*noun*)	3		could	123	1a2
coöperate	4		couldn't	21	3b
coöperation	6		couldst	25	3a
coöperative	5		council	34	2b
cope	7		counsel	26	3a
coping (*noun*)	5		counsellor	5	
copper	30	2b	count	66	1b
copperas	5		countenance	18	4a
copse	6		counter	13	5a
copy	38	2a	counterfeit	4	
coral	13	5a	countess	3	
cord	23	3a	countless	8	
cordial	20	3b	country	110	1a3
corduroy	4		county	27	3a
core	7		couple	29	2b
cork	11	5b	coupling	6	
corn	78	1a5	coupon	4	
corner	69	1b	courage	32	2b
coronation	6		courageous	8	
corporal	8		course	91	1a4
corporation	11	5b	court	62	1b
corps	5		courteous	12	5a
corpse	9		courtesy	12	5a
correct	39	2a	courtier	14	4b
correction	8		cousin	40	2a
correspond	14	4b	cove	6	
correspondence	14	4b	covenant	10	5b
correspondent	6		cover	98	1a3
corrupt	14	4b	covert	11	5b
corruption	8		covet	11	5b
corse	5		covetous	6	
corset	7		cow	54	1b
	70	1b	coward	20	3b
	26	3a	cowardice	7	
	10	5b	cowboy	4	
cot	16	4a	cowl	7	

cowslip	6			creed	6	
Cox	8			creek	16	4a
coxcomb	6			creep	36	2a
coy	6			*(see also* crept)		
cozy	5			crêpe	8	
crab	14	4b		crept	19	3b
crack	33	2b		crescent	6	
cracker	8			crest	16	4a
crackle	11	5b		Crete	3	
cradle	22	3b		cretonne	6	
craft	13	5a		crevice	4	
craftsman	3			crew	29	2b
crafty	5			crib	9	
crag	8			cricket	15	4b
cram	9			cried	52	1b
cramp	6			crier	3	
cranberry	5			cries	16	4a
crane	7			*(see also* cry)		
crank	5			crime	28	3a
crash	17	4a		criminal	10	5b
crate	7			crimson	15	4b
cravat	8			cripple	14	4b
crave	18	4a		crisis	4	
craven	5			crisp	11	5b
crawl	22	3b		critic	12	5a
crayon	3			critical	5	
craze	11	5b		criticise	5	
crazy	12	5a		criticism	6	
creak	7			croak	12	5a
cream	39	2a		crochet	7	
creamery	5			crock	5	
creamy	5			Cromwell	8	
create	28	2b		crook	5	
creation	16	4a		crooked	16	4a
creative	3			crop	48	2a
creator	9			cross	88	1a4
creature	46	2a		crosswise	3	
credit	27	3a		crouch	11	5b
creditor	8			crow	30	2b
credulous	5			crowd	50	1b

crown	50	1b		curiosity	13	5a
crucify	4			curious	26	3a
crude	8			curl	28	2b
cruel	42	2a		curly	5	
cruelty	15	4b		currant	9	
cruise	3			current	34	2b
cruller	3			curse	29	2b
crumb	15	4b		curtain	38	2a
crumble	12	5a		curve	22	3b
crusade	5			cushion	21	3b
crush	28	2b		custard	5	
Crusoe	9			custody	7	
crust	16	4a		custom	37	2a
crutch	10	5b		customary	9	
cry	74	1b		customer	22	3b
crystal	17	4a		custom-house	4	
crystalline	3			cut	113	1a2
cu.	6			cute	6	
Cuba	16	4a		cutter	11	5b
cube	13	5a		cycle	3	
cubit	6			cylinder	11	5b
cuckoo	15	4b		cymbal	6	
cucumber	5			cypress	9	
cud	3			czar	8	
cuddle	7					
cudgel	5					
cue	4			dad	4	
cuff	18	4a		daddy	6	
cull	6			daffodil	6	
cultivate	24	3a		dagger	10	5b
cultivation	7			daily	35	2b
culture	9			dainty	14	4b
cunning	24	3a		dairy	20	3b
cup	60	1b		daisy (D)	25	3a
cupboard	13	5a		Dakota	6	
Cupid	9			dale	13	5a
cur	5			dam	18	4a
curb	14	4b		damage	19	3b
curd	4			Damascus	5	
cure	29	2b		dame	19	3b

damn	12	5a	daybreak	5	
damnation	5		daylight	19	3b
damp	20	3b	dayspring	4	
damsel	13	5a	daytime	11	5b
Dan	26	3a	daze	6	
dance	72	1b	dazzle	13	5a
dancer	7		deacon	4	
dandelion	7		dead	80	1a5
dandruff	3		deaden	4	
dandy	6		deadly	15	4b
Dane	5		deaf	22	3b
danger	48	2a	deafen	3	
dangerous	34	2b	deal	63	1b
dangle	8		dealer	15	4b
Daniel	15	4b	dealing (*noun*)	10	5b
Danish	6		dean	8	
Danube	4		dear	87	1a4
Danville	4		dearth	6	
dare	59	1b	death	82	1a5
daring	8		deathbed	5	
Darius	4		deathless	3	
dark	83	1a5	debase	5	
darken	16	4a	debate	20	3b
darkness	36	2a	Deborah	5	
darling	23	3a	debt	39	2a
darn	9		debtor	6	
dart	27	3a	Dec.	3	
dash	42	2a	decade	4	
dastard	4		decay	26	3a
data	3		decease	10	5b
date	49	1b	deceit	11	5b
daub	4		deceitful	7	
daughter	64	1b	deceive	28	2b
dauntless	6		deceiver	5	
Dauphin	4		December	41	2a
davenport	4		decent	8	
David	22	3b	decide	55	1b
Davis	6		decidedly	6	
dawn	41	2a	decimal	3	
day	176	1a1	decision	18	4a

decisive	4	
deck	33	2b
declaration	6	
declare	48	2a
declension	4	
decline	23	3a
decorate	9	
decoration	12	5a
decoy	5	
decrease	16	4a
decree	18	4a
dedicate	12	5a
dedication	4	
deed	46	2a
deem	20	3b
deep	91	1a4
deepen	10	5b
deer	25	3a
deface	4	
default	3	
defeat	21	3b
defect	13	5a
defective	5	
defence (*see* defense)		
defend	28	2b
defendant	3	
defender	3	
defense	26	3a
defenseless	3	
defensive	3	
defer	6	
defiance	13	5a
deficiency	5	
defile	10	5b
define	7	
definite	9	
definition	5	
deform(ed)	8	
deformity	4	
defraud	5	
defy	19	3b
degenerate	7	
degrade	8	
degree	43	2a
deign	10	
deity	8	
dejected	6	
Delaware	9	
delay	41	2a
delegate	11	5b
deliberate	8	
deliberation	5	
delicacy	4	
delicate	25	3a
delicious	15	4b
delight	58	1b
delightful	20	3b
deliver	45	2a
deliverance	12	5a
deliverer	6	
delivery	15	4b
dell	9	
delta	8	
delude	5	
deluge	5	
delusion	5	
demand	50	1b
demeanor	5	
democracy	5	
democrat	8	
democratic	4	
demolish	4	
demon	7	
demonstrate	8	
demonstration	7	
demonstrative	5	
den	25	3a
denial	3	
Denmark	9	
denote	5	

denounce	9		desist	4	
dense	18	4a	desk	38	2a
dental	3		desolate	14	4b
dentist	4		desolation	11	5b
Denver	5		despair	25	3a
deny	31	2b	despatch	8	
depart	40	2a	desperate	17	4a
department	26	3a	desperation	3	
departure	10	5b	despise	24	3a
depend	35	2b	despite	14	4b
dependant	5		despondency	4	
dependence	5		dessert	7	
dependency	3		destination	6	
dependent	5		destine	14	4b
deplore	7		destiny	13	5a
deportment	5		destitute	7	
depose	6		destroy	50	1b
deposit	22	3b	destroyer	3	
depot	11	5b	destruction	23	3a
depress	5		destructive	3	
deprive	11	5b	detach	4	
depth	26	3a	detail	16	4a
depute	4		detain	15	4b
deputy	10	5b	detect	9	
deride	6		detective	3	
derision	7		detector	4	
derive	15	4b	determinate	4	
descend	33	2b	determination	7	
descendant	7		determine	33	2b
descent	12	5a	detest	6	
describe	40	2a	detestable	4	
description	22	3b	Detroit	5	
descry	9		develop	24	3a
desert	41	2a	development	17	4a
deserve	29	2b	device	14	4b
design	26	3a	devil	28	2b
designate	6		devilish	6	
desirable	12	5a	devote	26	3a
desire	59	1b	devotion	12	5a
desirous	9		devour	18	4a

devout	9	
dew	32	2b
dewdrop	4	
dewy	7	
diadem	5	
diagonal	3	
diagram	5	
dial	9	
dialogue	7	
diameter	4	
diamond	37	2a
Diana	9	
diaper	3	
diary	5	
dice	8	
Dick	28	2b
Dicky	7	
dictate	12	5a
dictionary	7	
did	140	1a2
didn't	25	3a
Dido	4	
die	102	1a3
diet	11	5b
differ	22	3b
difference	50	1b
different	63	1b
difficult	37	2a
difficulty	23	3a
diffuse	10	5b
dig	31	2b
digest	7	
digger	7	
dignify (ied)	11	5b
dignity	18	4a
dike	3	
dilapidated	4	
dilate	8	
diligence	6	
diligent	12	5a

dilute	3	
dim	25	3a
dime	15	4b
dimension	7	
diminish	12	5a
dimple	8	
din	13	5a
dine	34	2b
dinner	70	1b
dip	25	3a
diploma	5	
diplomat	4	
dipper	10	5b
dire	10	5b
direct	62	1b
direction	47	2a
director	15	4b
dirt	21	3b
dirty	21	3b
disagree	5	
disagreeable	9	
disappear	32	2b
disappoint	20	3b
disappointment	14	4b
disapprove	4	
disarm	7	
disaster	11	5b
disastrous	4	
disc	4	
(see also disk)		
discard	3	
discern	16	4a
discharge	20	3b
disciple	6	
discipline	12	5a
disclaim	4	
disclose	13	5a
discomfit	3	
discontent	16	4a
discontinue	4	

discord	9		disperse	14	4b
discordant	4		displace	4	
discount	4		display	26	3a
discourage	16	4a	displease	14	4b
discourse	12	5a	displeasure	7	
discover	49	1b	disposal	9	
discovery	23	3a	dispose	24	3a
discredit	3		disposition	12	5a
discreet	8		dispossess	3	
discretion	6		dispute	26	3a
discuss	18	4a	disqualify	4	
discussion	10	5b	disquiet(ed)	4	
disdain	15	4b	disregard	4	
disdainful	4		dissatisfy (ied)	3	
disease	35	2b	dissembler	3	
disfigure	5		dissension	6	
disgrace	19	3b	dissent	4	
disgraceful	3		dissipate	3	
disguise	19	3b	dissolution	6	
disgust(ed)	10	5b	dissolve	21	3b
dish	48	2a	dissuade	4	
dishonest	6		distaff	5	
dishonesty	5		distance	60	1b
dishonor	13	5a	distant	36	2a
disinfect	3		distemper	7	
disinherit	3		distil	9	
disk	4		distinct	25	3a
dislike	11	5b	distinction	11	5b
dismal	15	4b	distinguish	21	3b
dismay	16	4a	distinguished	3	
dismiss	22	3b	distort	4	
dismount	8		distract	10	5b
disobedience	4		distraction	3	
disobedient	5		distress	24	3a
disobey	13	5a	distribute	13	5a
disorder	11	5b	distribution	12	5a
disown	5		district	29	2b
dispatch	6		distrust	6	
dispel	4		disturb	26	3a
dispense	12	5a	disturbance	8	

ditch	27	3a	domestic	26	3a
ditty	5		dominate	3	
dive	14	4b	domination	4	
divers	7		dominion	15	4b
diverse	5		domino	6	
diversity	4		don (D)	7	
divert	7		Donald	9	
divide	67	1b	done	98	1a3
dividend	7		donkey	17	4a
divider	5		don't	50	1b
dividing	3		doom	22	3b
divination	4		door	107	1a3
divine	29	2b	doorstep	4	
divinity	8		doorway	7	
division	26	3a	Dora	7	
divisor	5		dormitory	3	
divorce	14	4b	Dorothy	13	5a
divulge	3		dose	7	
dizzy	9		dost	19	3b
do	180	1a1	dot	30	2b
docile	3		dotage	4	
dock	16	4a	dote	7	
doctor	51	1b	doth	25	3a
doctrine	14	4b	double	49	1b
document	8		doublet	4	
dodge	6		doubt	60	1b
doe	6		doubtful	16	4a
doer	6		doubtless	19	3b.
does	101	1a3	dough	8	
doesn't	22	3b	doughnut	5	
dog	73	1b	Douglas	5	
dogma	4		dove	24	3a
doily	4		dower	4	
doings	21	3b	down	144	1a2
doleful	6		downcast	3	
doll	28	2b	downright	3	
dollar	46	2a	downstairs	7	
dolly (D)	13	5a	downwards	22	3b
domain	4		downy	5	
dome	14	4b	dowry	4	

doz.	7		drip	18	4a
doze	5		drive	86	1a4
dozen	43	2a	driver	16	4a
Dr.	11	5b	drizzle	4	
drab	4		droll	4	
draft	27	3a	droop	23	3a
drag	30	2b	drop	75	1a
dragon	22	3b	dross	5	
drain	30	2b	drought	5	
drainage	6		drove	31	2b
Drake	7		drown	39	2a
dram	5		drowsiness	3	
drama	11	5b	drowsy	16	4a
dramatic	4		drudge	3	
drank	15	4b	drug	22	3b
drape	6		drum	33	2b
drapery	7		drunk	14	4b
draught	17	4a	drunkard	7	
draw	89	1a4	drunken	11	5b
drawback	3		drunkenness	5	
drawbridge	4		dry	69	1b
drawer	16	4a	Dryden	5	
drawn	15	4b	duchess	7	
dread	34	2b	duck	35	2b
dreadful	33	2b	due	41	2a
dream	69	1b	duel	5	
dreamland	4		dug	19	3b
dreary	11	5b	duke	22	3b
dreg	4		dull	25	3a
drench	6		dulness	5	
dress	99	1a3	duly	8	
dresser	8		dumb	23	3a
dressmaker	5		dump	6	
drew	36	2a	dunce	8	
dried	18	4a	dung	5	
drier	6		dungeon	14	4b
drift	17	4a	dunghill	5	
driftwood	3		dupe	4	
drill	29	2b	duplicate	5	
drink	79	1a5	durable	7	

duration	4		easily	31	2b
during	96	1a3	east	75	1a5
durst	8		Easter	16	4a
dusk	10	5b	eastern	27	3a
dusky	9		eastward	9	
dust	51	1b	easy	68	1b
duster	6		eat	88	1a4
dusty	14	4b	eaves	10	5b
Dutch	26	3a	ebb	10	5b
Dutchman	4		eccentric	5	
duty	57	1b	echo	28	2b
dwarf	14	4b	eclipse	8	
dwell	34	2b	economic	3	
dweller	5		economical	6	
dwelling	22	3b	economist	6	
dwelling-place	4		economy	6	
dwelt	17	4a	ecstasy	9	
dwindle	8		eddy	7	
dye	17	4a	Eden	13	5a
dying	23	3a	Edgar	6	
dynamite	3		edge	53	1b
			edging	4	
each	142	1a2	edifice	11	5b
eager	33	2b	edify	6	
eagle	28	2b	Edith	11	5b
ear	77	1a5	edition	9	
earl	14	4b	editor	5	
earldom	4		Edmund	5	
early	92	1a4	educate	8	
earn	47	2a	education	23	3a
earnest	30	2b	educational	5	
earnestness	3		Edward	26	3a
earning	4		Edwin	6	
earth	84	1a5	eel	4	
earthen	6		e'er	18	4a
earthenware	5		efface	4	
earthly	20	3b	effect	47	2a
earthquake	15	4b	effective	7	
ease	35	2b	effectual	7	
easier	14	4b	efficiency	4	

efficient	5		Ellen	10	5b
effort	33	2b	elm	21	3b
egg	78	1a5	eloquence	12	5a
Egypt	23	3a	eloquent	5	
Egyptian	11	5b	Elsa	6	
eight	70	1b	else	60	1b
eighteen	30	2b	elsewhere	17	4a
eighteenth	8		Elsie	5	
eighth	26	3a	elves	8	
eighty	22	3b	Elysian	4	
either	70	1b	'em	9	
eke	4		emancipation	4	
elaborate	6		embark	5	
elapse	4		embarrass	6	
elastic	10	5b	embassy	7	
elate	30	2b	embattled	6	
elbow	19	3b	ember	3	
elder	19	3b	emblem	3	
eldest	18	4a	embody	6	
Eleanor	6		emboss	4	
elect	41	2a	embrace	25	3a
election	23	3a	embroider	10	5b
elector	6		embroidery	11	5b
electric	23	3a	emerald	6	
electrical	8		emerge	8	
electricity	5		emergency	6	
elegance	3		emery	4	
elegant	14	4b	emigrant	4	
element	21	3b	emigrate	5	
elephant	19	3b	emigration	4	
elevate	14	4b	Emily	9	
elevation	8		eminence	6	
elevator	7		eminent	9	
eleven	28	2b	emit	4	
eleventh	8		Emma	7	
elf	13	5a	emotion	11	5b
Elijah	4		emperor	24	3a
Elizabeth	19	3b	emphasize	5	
ell	4		emphatic	3	
Ella	11	5b	empire	32	2b

employ	37	2a		Englander	18	4a
employee	15	4b		English	57	1b
employer	7			Englishman	18	4a
employment	11	5b		engrave	6	
empress	8			engraver	3	
emptiness	3			engross	4	
empty	44	2a		enhance	4	
enable	15	4b		enjoin	8	
enact	7			enjoy	8	
enamel	9			enjoyment	7	
enamor(ed)	4			enlarge	17	4a
encamp	9			enlargement	3	
enchant	13	5a		enlighten	7	
enchantment	7			enlist	9	
enclose	21	3b		enmity	9	
encompass	4			ennoble	8	
encounter	20	3b		enormous	25	3a
encourage	25	3a		enough	104	1a3
encouragement	3			enquire	9	
end	126	1a2		enrage	8	
endanger	3			enrich	13	5a
endear	6			enroll	8	
endeavor	17	4a		enrollment	4	
ending (*noun*)	13	5a		ensign	9	
endless	17	4a		enslave	3	
endow	10	5b		ensnare	4	
endue	9			ensue	13	5a
endurance	3			entangle	8	
endure	27	3a		enter	70	1b
enemy	55	1b		enterprise	13	5a
energetic	5			enterprising	3	
energy	15	4b		entertain	27	3a
enfold	3			entertainment	12	5a
enforce	10	5b		enthrone	4	
engage	29	2b		enthusiasm	11	5b
engagement	12	5a		enthusiast	3	
engender	4			enthusiastic	8	
engine	35	2b		entice	12	5a
engineer	16	4a		entire	51	1b
England	60	1b		entitle	16	4a

entrails	5		eschew	4	
entrance	29	2b	escort	9	
entreat	11	5b	escutcheon	5	
entreaty	5		Eskimo	4	
entrust	5		especial	48	2a
entry	17	4a	espouse	7	
envelop	3		espy	6	
envelope	16	4a	essay	8	
envious	12	5a	essence	8	
environ(s)	4		essential	11	5b
envy	27	3a	establish	37	2a
Ephesus	5		establishment	11	5b
epic	3		estate	26	3a
epidemic	5		esteem	21	3b
Episcopal	5		estimate	17	4a
episode	4		estimation	6	
epistle	4		estrange	4	
epitaph	6		etc.	15	4b
epoch	4		eternal	27	3a
equal	60	1b	eternity	12	5a
equality	9		Ethel	4	
equator	8		ethereal	7	
equip	12	5a	eunuch	7	
equipage	4		Euphrates	5	
equipment	8		Europe	38	2a
equity	8		European	16	4a
equivalent	6		Eva	4	
era	6		evade	3	
eraser	5		evaporate	4	
ere	40	2a	eve (E)	27	3a
erect	30	2b	even	117	1a2
erection	4		evening	74	1b
Erie	7		event	41	2a
Erin	4		eventide	4	
err	21	3b	eventual	4	
errand	16	4a	ever	117	1a2
error	30	2b	evergreen	7	
eruption	3		everlasting	19	3b
Esau	4		evermore	11	5b
escape	49	1b	every	151	1a1

everybody	33	2b		execute	17	4a
everyday	7			execution	10	5b
everyone	19	3b		executioner	6	
everything	61	1b		executive	11	5b
everywhere	27	3a		executor	6	
evidence	19	3b		exempt	8	
evident	20	3b		exercise	51	1b
evil	44	2a		exert	4	
evildoer	4			exertion	5	
evince	5			Exeter	6	
evolution	3			exhalation	4	
ewe	14	4b		exhale	6	
exact	48	2a		exhaust	17	4a
exaggerate	7			exhibit	16	4a
exalt	15	4b		exhibition	9	
examination	21	3b		exhort	5	
examine	33	2b		exhortation	5	
examiner	6			exile	15	4b
example	41	2a		exist	17	4a
exasperate	3			existence	14	4b
exceed	25	3a		expand	8	
exceeding	12	5a		expanse	4	
excel	14	4b		expansion	6	
excellence	7			expansive	3	
excellency	5			expect	56	1b
excellent	37	2a		expectant	6	
except	68	1b		expectation	13	5a
exception	18	4a		expedient	7	
exceptional	8			expedition	16	4a
excess	18	4a		expel	11	5b
excessive	10	5b		expend	5	
exchange	33	2b		expenditure	4	
excite	24	3a		expense	33	2b
excitement	11	5b		expensive	16	4a
exclaim	27	3a		experience	40	2a
exclamation	6			experiment	12	5a
exclude	7			expert	14	4b
exclusive	14	4b		expire	16	4a
excursion	8			explain	39	2a
excuse	31	2b		explanation	10	5b

exploit	11	5b		fabric	8	
exploration	10	5b		face	107	1a3
explore	15	4b		facility	5	
explorer	6			fact	54	1b
explosion	5			faction	8	
export	10	5b		factor	6	
expose	22	3b		factory	26	3a
exposition	5			faculty	12	5a
exposure	3			fade	35	2b
express	55	1b		fail	46	2a
expression	13	5a		failure	13	5a
expressive	4			fain	8	
expressly	3			faint	36	2a
exquisite	11	5b		fair	114	1a2
extend	51	1b		fairy	34	2b
extension	12	5a		fairyland	11	5b
extensive	13	5a		faith	41	2a
extent	16	4a		faithful	43	2a
exterior	7			faithfulness	5	
external	4			faithless	8	
extinct	5			falcon	8	
extinguish	8			fall	126	1a2
extinguisher	3			fallen	20	3b
extol	8			fallow	5	
extra	17	4a		false	35	2b
extract	11	5b		falsehood	14	4b
extraordinary	14	4b		falter	10	5b
extravagance	3			fame	33	2b
extravagant	7			familiar	30	2b
extreme	31	2b		family	83	1a5
extremity	8			famine	22	3b
exult	7			famish	5	
eye	120	1a2		famous	50	1b
eyeball	4			fan	33	2b
eyebrow	9			fancy	49	1b
eyelet	4			Fannie	11	5b
eyelid	10	5b		fantastic	8	
eyesight	5			fantasy	4	
				far	115	1a2
fable	17	4a		far-away	3	

farce	7		feature	28	2b
fare	38	2a	February	30	2b
farewell	28	2b	fed	30	2b
farm	67	1b	federal	10	5b
farmer	59	1b	federation	5	
farmhouse	6		fee	16	4a
farmyard	7		feeble	22	3b
far-off	9		feed	63	1b
farther	40	2a	feeder	8	
farthest	13	5a	feel	88	1a4
farthing	5		feeling	48	2a
fascinate	5		feet	82	1a5
fashion	43	2a	feign	17	4a
fashionable	9		Felix	5	
fast	79	1a5	fell	67	1b
fasten	33	2b	fellow	65	1b
fat	50	1b	fellowship	12	5a
fatal	21	3b	felon	5	
fate	32	2b	felt	57	1b
father	114	1a2	female	25	3a
fatherland	3		feminine	9	
fatherless	5		fen	6	
fathom	9		fence	49	1b
fatigue	8		fender	5	
fatness	3		Ferdinand	5	
faucet	3		fern	14	4b
fault	36	2a	ferocious	4	
faultless	4		ferry	13	5a
faulty	5		fertile	16	4a
favor	51	1b	fertility	4	
favorable	22	3b	fertilize	9	
favorite	29	2b	fertilizer	8	
fawn	7		fervent	4	
fealty	5		fervor	6	
fear	79	1a5	festal	5	
fearful	24	3a	festival	14	4b
fearless	11	5b	festive	5	
feast	41	2a	festivity	3	
feat	12	5a	fetch	28	2b
feather	45	2a	fetter	11	5b

feud	6		financial	11	5b
fever	33	2b	find	131	1a2
few	99	1a3	fine	108	1a3
fib	3		fineness	5	
fiber	13	5a	finger	54	1b
fickle	8		finish	72	1b
fiction	9		fir	16	4a
fiddle	9		fire	111	1a3
fidelity	5		firearms	5	
Fido	4		firebrand	6	
fie	5		firefly	4	
field	92	1a4	fireman	7	
fiend	12	5a	fireplace	10	5b
fierce	41	2a	fireproof	4	
fierceness	5		fireside	7	
fiery	21	3b	firm	53	1b
fife	8		firmament	10	5b
fifteen	43	2a	firmness	5	
fifteenth	10	5b	first	136	1a2
fifth	42	2a	first-born	8	
fiftieth	4		fish	66	1b
fifty	46	2a	fisher	10	5b
fig	15	4b	fisherman	15	4b
fight	69	1b	fishhook	3	
fighter	8		fist	20	3b
figure	68	1b	fit	68	1b
file	26	3a	fitness	6	
filer	3		five	101	1a3
filial	6		fix	55	1b
fill	94	1a4	fixture	7	
filler	5		flag	43	2a
fillet	5		flake	13	5a
film	10	5b	flame	36	2a
filth	7		Flanders	4	
filthiness	3		flange	4	
filthy	10	5b	flank	10	5b
fin	7		flannel	9	
final	40	2a	flannelette	4	
finally	40	2a	flap	13	5a
finance	7		flare	5	

flash	38	2a		flop	3	
flask	4			Flora	4	
flat	44	2a		Florence	10	5b
flatten	3			Florida	13	5a
flatter	26	3a		floss	6	
flatterer	4			flounce	4	
flattery	11	5b		flounder	6	
flaunt	5			flour	39	2a
flavor	14	4b		flourish	20	3b
flaw	6			flow	59	1b
flax	16	4a		flower	94	1a4
flaxen	3			floweret	6	
flay	4			flowerpot	3	
flea	4			flowery	15	4b
flecked	4			flown	4	
fled	25	3a		flue	3	
flee	22	3b		flush	4	
fleece	15	4b		fluid	15	4b
fleecy	7			flung	14	4b
fleet	34	2b		flute	11	5b
flesh	40	2a		flutter	23	3a
fleshy	4			fly	76	1a5
Fletcher	4			foam	22	3b
flew	33	2b		fob	3	
flexible	7			fodder	9	
flicker	4			foe	30	2b
flies	24	3a		fog	17	4a
flight	29	2b		foggy	6	
flimsy	4			foil	11	5b
fling	14	4b		fold	42	2a
flint	11	5b		folder	5	
flinty	4			foliage	9	
flirt	8			folk	44	2a
flit	12	5a		follow	109	1a3
float	33	2b		follower	15	4b
flock	34	2b		following	54	1b
flog	3			folly	27	3a
flood	34	2b		fond	39	2a
floor	79	1a5		fondness	3	
flooring	4			food	78	1a5

fool	49	1b	forgave	5	
foolish	34	2b	forge	15	4b
foolishness	4		forgery	3	
foot	99	1a3	forget	65	1b
football	10	5b	forgetfulness	7	
footman	9		forgive	27	3a
footprint	3		forgiveness	11	5b
footsteps	14	4b	forgot	31	2b
footstool	4		forgotten	29	2b
for	201	1a1	fork	29	2b
forbade	6		forlorn	12	5a
forbear	11	5b	form	98	1a3
forbearance	5		formal	9	
forbid	28	2b	formation	8	
forbidden	15	4b	former	52	1b
force	64	1b	formidable	5	
forcible	6		fornication	4	
ford (F)	18	4a	forsake	19	3b
fore	13	5a	forsook	7	
forearm	3		forsworn	4	
forecast	3		fort	29	2b
forefather	8		forth	59	1b
forego	7		forthwith	11	5b
foregone	3		fortieth	3	
forehead	32	2b	fortification	3	
foreign	42	2a	fortify	8	
foreigner	18	4a	fortitude	6	
foreman	4		fortnight	7	
foremost	15	4b	fortress	15	4b
forenoon	17	4a	fortunate	20	3b
forerunner	3		fortune	44	2a
foresee	11	5b	forty	48	2a
foresight	3		forward	52	1b
forest	63	1b	foster	11	5b
foretell	4		fought	38	2a
foretold	9		foul	27	3a
forever	20	3b	found	114	1a2
forewarn	4		foundation	26	3a
forfeit	13	5a	founder	15	4b
forfeiture	4		fount	7	

fountain	31	2b		freight	24	3a
four	114	1a2		French	57	1b
fourfold	3			Frenchman	8	
fourscore	7			frenzy	8	
fourteen	22	3b		frequent	37	2a
fourteenth	5			fresh	79	1a5
fourth	52	1b		freshman	4	
fowl	23	3a		freshness	7	
fowler	4			fret	25	3a
fox	39	2a		fretful	6	
fraction	13	5a		friar	10	5b
fragment	10	5b		Friday	36	2a
fragrance	11	5b		fried	7	
fragrant	14	4b		friend	106	1a3
frail	20	3b		friendly	37	2a
frailty	8			friendship	28	2b
frame	38	2a		fright	28	2b
framework	4			frighten	33	2b
franc	3			frightful	9	
France	49	1b		frill	4	
Frances	7			fringe	14	4b
Francis	14	4b		frisk	4	
frank (F)	34	2b		frisky	3	
Frankfort	7			Fritz	10	5b
Franklin	10	5b		fro	16	4a
frantic	6			frock	13	5a
fraternal	8			frog	23	3a
fraternity	6			frolic	13	5a
fraud	11	5b		from	195	1a1
fraught	7			front	81	1a5
fray	8			frontier	8	
freak	4			frost	45	2a
freckle	8			frosty	12	5a
Fred	18	4a		froth	3	
Frederick	8			froward	8	
Fredericksburg	4			frown	21	3b
free	86	1a4		froze	7	
freedom	43	2a		frozen	28	2b
freeman	10	5b		frugal	6	
freeze	30	2b		fruit	75	1b

fruitful	14	4b	Gabriel	4	
fruitless	7		gad (G)	7	
frustrate	6		gag	3	
fry	13	5a	gaiety	5	
ft.	17	4a	gaily	7	
fudge	3		gain	52	1b
fuel	20	3b	'gainst	6	
fugitive	13	5a	gait	10	5b
fulfil	18	4a	gaiter	5	
full	108	1a3	gal.	8	
fully	23	3a	gale	16	4a
fulness	13	5a	Galilee	5	
Fulton	10	5b	gall	12	5a
fumble	3		gallant	18	4a
fume	10	5b	gallantry	3	
fun	39	2a	gallery	18	4a
function	13	5a	gallon	11	5b
fund	15	4b	gallop	22	3b
fundamental	5		gallows	13	5a
funeral	27	3a	galvanize	3	
funnel	3		gamble	4	
funny	27	3a	gambol	5	
fur	47	2a	game	69	1b
furious	21	3b	gander	4	
furnace	20	3b	gang	11	5b
furnish	43	2a	gap	16	4a
furniture	32	2b	gape	8	
furrow	12	5a	garage	8	
furry	4		garb	5	
further	42	2a	garbage	4	
furthermore	8		garden	86	1a4
fury	22	3b	gardener	19	3b
fuse	5		garland	18	4a
fuss	7		garlic	3	
future	43	2a	garment	29	2b
futurity	4		garner	4	
			garnish	7	
			garret	6	
gabble	5		garrison	9	
gaberdine	7		garter	9	

gas	23	3a		germ	9	
gash	7			German	39	2a
gasp	9			Germany	28	2b
gate	64	1b		gesture	8	
gateway	8			get	136	1a2
gather	67	1b		geyser	4	
gaudy	4			ghastly	9	
gauge	3			ghost	31	2b
gaunt	8			ghostly	6	
gauntlet	5			giant	38	2a
gauze	6			giddy	7	
gave	92	1a4		gift	55	1b
gay	39	2a		gig	6	
gaze	28	2b		gigantic	6	
gear	7			Gilbert	5	
geese	15	4b		gild	19	3b
gelatin	5			gill	7	
gem	28	2b		gilt	6	
gender	4			gin	8	
general	81	1a5		ginger	11	5b
generation	20	3b		gingerbread	9	
generosity	7			gingham	8	
generous	28	2b		gipsy	6	
genial	14	4b		gird	12	5a
genius	17	4a		girdle	16	4a
Genoa	5			girl	98	1a3
gentile	6			girt	9	
gentle	62	1b		girth	6	
gentleman	59	1b		give	145	1a2
gentleness	10	5b		given	96	1a3
gentlewoman	4			giver	9	
gently	21	3b		glacier	8	
genuine	13	5a		glad	79	1a5
geographer	5			gladden	4	
geographical	4			glade	10	5b
geography	16	4a		gladness	10	5b
geometry	5			glance	32	2b
George	45	2a		gland	3	
georgette (G)	6			glare	18	4a
Georgia	10	5b		glass	70	1b

gasoline 11 5b

glassful	4		godlike	7	
glassware	5		godly	5	
glassy	5		godmother	10	5b
gleam	18	4a	goes	29	2b
glean	10	5b	going	63	1b
glee	13	5a	gold	91	1a4
glen	13	5a	golden	55	1b
glide	21	3b	goldsmith	6	
glimmer	9		golf	6	
glimpse	13	5a	gone	64	1b
glisten	12	5a	gong	3	
glitter	24	3a	good	168	1a1
globe	28	2b	good-by	20	3b
gloom	17	4a	goodliness	5	
gloomy	12	5a	goodly	21	3b
glorify	11	5b	goodman	6	
glorious	31	2b	goodness	26	3a
glory	44	2a	goodwill	7	
gloss	5		goody	9	
glossy	6		goose	38	2a
glove	35	2b	gore	11	5b
glow	30	2b	gorge	9	
glue	10	5b	gorgeous	14	4b
glutton	3		gospel	15	4b
gnash	5		gossip	9	
gnat	8		got	82	1a5
gnaw	13	5a	Goth	4	
go	160	1a1	Gothic	10	5b
goad	4		gotten	4	
goal	14	4b	gourd	5	
goat	47	2a	govern	28	2b
gobble	9		government	62	1b
gobbler	4		governor	37	2a
goblet	8		gown	31	2b
goblin	5		grab	6	
gocart	3		grace (G)	59	1b
God	81	1a5	graceful	17	4a
goddess	19	3b	gracious	24	3a
godfather	3		gradation	4	
godhead	5		grade	31	2b

gradual	28	3a		gravy	8	
graduate	17	4a		gray (G)	56	1b
graduation	4			grayheaded	4	
graft	5			graze	22	3b
grail	4			grease	11	5b
grain	58	1b		great	159	1a1
grammar	13	5a		greatness	18	4a
grammatical	3			Grecian	7	
granary	4			Greece	13	5a
grand	42	2a		greediness	4	
grandchild	3			greedy	17	4a
grandchildren	3			Greek	22	3b
granddaughter	3			green (G)	81	1a5
grandeur	5			greenhouse	3	
grandfather	25	3a		Greenland	3	
grandma	18	4a		greenness	3	
grandmother	31	2b		Greenwich	3	
grandpa	16	4a		greenwood	4	
grandparents	3			greet	36	2a
grandsire	7			grew	55	1b
grandson	7			grey (G)	20	3b
grange	8			greyhound	7	
granite	11	5b		griddle	5	
grant	51	1b		grief	29	2b
granulate	4			grievance	5	
grape	37	2a		grieve	25	3a
graphite	4			grievous	12	5a
grapple	4			grim	13	5a
grasp	19	3b		grimace	4	
grass	64	1b		grin	15	4b
grasshopper	16	4a		grind	29	2b
grassy	7			grinder	4	
grate	18	4a		grindstone	6	
grateful	28	3a		grip	14	4b
gratify	7			gripe	6	
gratitude	16	4a		grit	4	
grave	49	1b		groan	28	3a
gravel	10	5b		grocer	17	4a
graven	5			grocery	9	
gravity	7			groom	11	5b

groove	8		gun	39	2a
grope	9		gunpowder	10	5b
gross	18	4a	gurgle	3	
grot	4		gush	12	5a
grotesque	4		gust	8	
ground	90	1a4	gut	3	
group	33	2b	gutter	10	5b
grove	29	2b	gymnasium	8	
grovel	4		gymnastics	5	
grow(n)	94	1a4	gypsy	6	
grower	3				
growl	13	5a	ha	26	3a
growth	28	3a	habit	28	3a
grub	6		habitation	10	5b
grudge	10	5b	habitual	3	
gruel	4		hack	9	
gruff	12	5a	hackney	5	
grumble	13	5a	had	172	1a1
grunt	3		haddock	4	
guarantee	10	5b	hadn't	4	
guard	50	1b	hadst	16	4a
guardian	10	5b	hag	3	
guess	57	1b	Hagar	6	
guest	38	2a	Hague	3	
guidance	4		hail	30	2b
guide	50	1b	hailstone	3	
guidepost	4		hair	84	1a5
guilder	4		hairy	6	
guile	7		Haiti	6	
guilt	16	4a	hale	8	
guiltless	12	5a	half	126	1a2
guilty	23	3a	hall	66	1b
guinea	10	5b	halloo	9	
Guinivere	4		hallow	13	5a
guise	5		Hallowe'en	4	
guitar	5		halt	18	4a
gulf	29	2b	halter	7	
gull	6		halve	5	
gully	3		ham	19	3b
gum	10	5b	Hamilton	16	4a

hamlet (H)	15	4b	Harlem	5	
hammer	33	2b	harlot	10	5b
hammock	6		harm	39	2a
Hampshire	4		harmless	13	5a
hand	148	1a2	harmonious	7	
handful	15	4b	harmony	21	3b
handiwork	4		harness	23	3a
handkerchief	32	2b	Harold	13	5a
handle	43	2a	harp	19	3b
handmade	5		Harrison	7	
handsome	31	2b	harrow	9	
handwriting	3		harry (H)	37	2a
handy	7		harsh	19	3b
hang	71	1b	harshness	3	
hanger	5		hart	13	5a
hangman	5		Harvard	5	
Hannah	8		harvest	44	2a
Hanover	6		has	146	1a2
Hans	14	4b	hasn't	9	
hap	7		hast	21	3b
hapless	8		haste	37	2a
haply	9		hasten	31	2b
happen	63	1b	hastily	12	5a
happily	17	4a	hasty	14	4b
happiness	35	2b	hat	67	1b
happy	88	1a4	hatch	13	5a
harass	4		hatchet	12	5a
harbinger	5		hate	45	2a
harbor	32	2b	hateful	11	5a
hard	103	1a3	hath	16	4a
harden	15	4b	hatred	18	4a
hardhearted	3		Hattie	4	
hardihood	3		haughty	18	4a
hardly	43	2a	haul	13	5a
hardness	6		haunch(es)	5	
hardship	12	5a	Havana	7	
hardware	10	5b	have	194	1a1
hardy	17	4a	haven	10	5b
hare	20	3b	havoc	7	
hark	21	3b	hawk	22	3b

haunt 22 3b

hawthorn	6		Hebrew	7	
hay	47	2a	Hebron	4	
haycock	5		Hector	6	
hazard	7		he'd	7	
haze	5		hedge	25	3a
hazel (H)	10	5b	hedgehog	8	
he	194	1a1	hedgerow	4	
head	132	1a2	heed	21	3b
headache	9		heedless	6	
headlight	3		heel	45	2a
headlong	13	5a	heifer	11	5b
headquarters	10	5b	height	54	1b
headstrong	3		heinous	5	
heal	25	3a	heir	21	3b
health	49	1b	held	71	1b
healthful	10	5b	Helen	19	3b
healthy	16	4a	hell	21	3b
heap	35	2b	he'll	5	
hear	114	1a2	hellish	3	
heard	74	1b	hello	11	5b
hearer	8		helm	13	5a
hearken	12	5a	helmet	15	4b
heart	92	1a4	help	109	1a3
hearted	9		helper	11	5b
heartfelt	4		helpful	10	5b
hearth	22	3b	helpless	18	4a
heartily	9		hem	16	4a
hearty	18	4a	hemisphere	9	
heat	62	1b	hemlock	6	
heater	5		hemstich	3	
heath	13	5a	hen	43	2a
heathen	16	4a	hence	37	2a
heather	4		henceforth	23	3a
heave	20	3b	henceforward	3	
heaven	56	1b	Henry	40	2a
heavenly	17	4a	her	161	1a1
heavenward	5		herald	13	5a
heavily	14	4b	herb	19	3b
heaviness	8		Herbert	8	
heavy	82	1a5	Hercules	7	

herd	29	2b		hill	88	1a4
herdsman	5			hillock	5	
here	155	1a1		hillside	17	4a
hereafter	14	4b		hilltop	4	
hereby	7			hilly	4	
hereditary	4			hilt	4	
herein	9			him	175	1a1
here's	6			himself	83	1a5
heresy	6			hind	23	3a
heretic	6			hinder	17	4a
heretofore	8			hinge	11	5b
herewith	7			hint	15	4b
heritage	7			hip	17	4a
hermit	10	5b		Hiram	5	
hero	32	2b		hire	35	2b
Herod	4			his	194	1a1
heroic	14	4b		hiss	19	3b
heroism	4			historian	6	
herring	6			historic	10	5b
hers	12	5a		historical	5	
herself	55	1b		history	49	1b
he's	9			hit	32	2b
hesitate	12	5a		hitch	5	
hesitation	3			hither	24	3a
hew	16	4a		hitherto	13	5a
hewer	3			hive	17	4a
hexagon	5			ho	16	4a
hey	5			hoar	7	
Hiawatha	10	5b		hoard	10	5b
hickory	5			hoarse	7	
hid	35	2b		hoary	10	5b
hidden	16	4a		hobble	3	
hide	58	1b		hobby	7	
hideous	8			hobgoblin	4	
hie	6			hock	4	
high	141	1a2		hockey	3	
highland	14	4b		hod	5	
highness	10	5b		hoe	14	4b
highroad	3			hog	21	3b
highway	18	4a		hoist	6	

hold	106	1a3	hornet	4	
holder	15	4b	horrible	20	3b
hole	60	1b	horrid	13	5a
holiday	35	2b	horror	19	3b
holiness	9		horse	108	1a3
Holland	15	4b	horseback	17	4a
hollow	43	2a	horsehair	3	
holly	8		horseman	21	3b
holy	39	2a	horseshoe	5	
homage	9		horseshoer	3	
home	128	1a2	hose	15	4b
homeless	4		hosiery	6	
homely	13	5a	hospitable	8	
Homer	9		hospital	25	3a
homesick	7		hospitality	7	
homeward	12	5a	host	30	2b
hominy	3		hostage	3	
hone	4		hostess	4	
honest	48	2a	hostile	11	5b
honesty	7		hostility	4	
honey	36	2a	hot	80	1a5
honeycomb	8		hotel	24	3a
honeymoon	3		hothouse	3	
honeysuckle	5		hound	15	4b
honor	60	1b	hour	105	1a3
honorable	25	3a	hourly	5	
hood	20	3b	house	147	1a2
hoof	25	3a	household	28	3a
hook	32	2b	housekeeper	8	
hoop	11	5b	housetop	9	
hoot	9		housewife	9	
hop	27	3a	housework	5	
hope	93	1a4	Houston	11	5b
hopeful	10	5b	hover	13	5a
hopeless	14	4b	how	171	1a1
hopper	4		Howard	9	
Horace	8		howbeit	4	
horizon	15	4b	Howe	6	
horizontal	7		howe'er	10	5b
horn	46	2a	however	75	1b

howl	27	3a
howsoever	4	
hr.	7	
hub	3	
Hubert	5	
huddle	5	
Hudson	20	3b
hue	13	5a
huff	4	
hug	11	5b
huge	36	2a
Hugh	7	
hulk	5	
hull	5	
hum	22	3b
human	39	2a
humane	6	
humanity	11	5b
humankind	3	
humble	28	3a
humbleness	4	
humiliation	4	
humility	10	5b
humor	23	3a
humorous	6	
hundred	97	1a3
hundredth	6	
hung	37	2a
Hungarian	5	
Hungary	4	
hunger	28	3a
hungry	40	2a
hunt	60	1b
hunter	29	2b
huntsman	6	
hurl	18	4a
hurrah	12	5a
hurray	3	
hurricane	5	
hurry	51	1b

hurt	55	1b
hurtful	4	
husband	55	1b
husbandman	5	
husbandry	7	
hush	26	3a
husk	8	
hustle	7	
hut	27	3a
hydrometer	4	
hymn	17	4a
hypocrisy	7	
hypocrite	9	
Hyssop	4	
hysterical	3	
I	138	1a2
ice	61	1b
iceberg	4	
Ichabod	5	
icy	15	4b
I'd	15	4b
Ida	4	
Idaho	3	
idea	46	2a
ideal	16	4a
identify	6	
idiot	13	5a
idle	35	2b
idleness	13	5a
idler	5	
idol	15	4b
idolatry	6	
if	178	1a1
ignoble	9	
ignorance	16	4a
ignorant	20	3b
ignore	3	
ill	59	1b
I'll	34	2b

illegal	4		imperative	7	
Illinois	12	5a	imperfect	12	5a
illness	11	5b	imperfection	3	
illuminate	7		imperial	17	4a
illumine	5		imperil	3	
illusion	5		imperious	5	
illustrate	13	5a	impersonal	3	
illustration	8		impetuous	6	
illustrious	11	5b	impious	9	
I'm	34	2b	implement	12	5a
image	23	3a	implore	10	5b
imaginable	4		imply	4	
imagination	21	3b	import	22	3b
imaginative	4		importance	27	3a
imagine	38	2a	important	54	1b
imbibe	4		importation	3	
imitate	14	4b	importer	4	
imitation	3		impose	16	4a
immeasurable	5		imposition	3	
immediate	38	2a	impossible	35	2b
immense	22	3b	impotent	4	
immigrant	4		impress	12	5a
immigration	3		impression	16	4a
imminent	4		impressive	3	
immortal	25	3a	imprison	13	5a
immortality	8		imprisonment	8	
immovable	5		improve	32	2b
immunity	3		improvement	14	4b
immutable	4		impudence	3	
Imogen	4		impudent	5	
imp	3		impulse	7	
impair	7		impure	4	
impart	14	4b	impute	8	
impartial	6		in	211	1a1
impatience	5		in.	10	5b
impatient	13	5a	inability	3	
impediment	6		inaccessible	3	
impel	7		inanimate	3	
impend	4		inasmuch	6	
impenetrable	3		incapable	5	

incense	16	4a		indignation	15	4b
incessant	7			indignity	5	
inch	51	1b		indigo	8	
incident	11	5b		indirect	7	
incidental	3			indispensable	4	
inclination	6			indistinct	3	
incline	25	3a		individual	24	3a
inclose	14	4b		indolence	3	
include	43	2a		indolent	3	
income	13	5a		indoors	9	
incomparable	4			induce	14	4b
incomplete	4			inducement	4	
inconstant	4			indulge	9	
inconvenience	8			indulgence	6	
increase	53	1b		industrial	3	
incredible	6			industrious	17	4a
incubator	4			industry	29	2b
incur	10	5b		inestimable	3	
incurable	6			inevitable	10	5b
Ind.	6			inexhaustible	3	
indebted	8			inexperienced	5	
indeed	65	1b		infallible	3	
indefinite	4			infamous	5	
indent	6			infamy	5	
independence	16	4a		infancy	8	
independent	25	3a		infant	19	3b
indescribable	5			infect	6	
index	8			infection	3	
India	23	3a		infectious	4	
Indian	67	1b		infer	5	
Indiana	10	5b		inferior	18	4a
Indianapolis	3			infernal	7	
indicate	30	2b		infest	4	
indication	4			infidel	5	
indicative	6			infinite	18	4a
indictment	4			infinitive	4	
Indies	10	5b		infirm	4	
indifference	4			infirmity	8	
indifferent	7			inflame	13	5a
indignant	8			inflammation	4	

inflict	11	5b	inquiry	10	5b
influence	30	2b	insane	5	
influential	3		inscribe	4	
inform	31	2b	inscription	7	
informal	5		insect	24	3a
information	26	3a	insensible	6	
infuse	6		insert	11	5b
infusion	3		insertion	6	
ingenious	9		inside	48	2a
inglorious	3		insight	3	
ingratitude	5		insignificant	8	
ingredient	8		insinuate	3	
inhabit	16	4a	insist	21	3b
inhabitant	13	5a	insole	4	
inherit	18	4a	insolence	3	
inheritance	13	5a	insolent	4	
inhospitable	3		insomuch	4	
inhuman	4		inspect	6	
iniquity	7		inspection	6	
initial	7		inspector	8	
injunction	5		inspiration	11	5b
injure	26	3a	inspire	14	4b
injurious	8		install	10	5b
injury	17	4a	installment	5	
injustice	9		instance	24	3a
ink	28	3a	instant	32	2b
inkwell	5		instead	58	1b
inlaid	5		instinct	13	5a
inlet	4		instinctive	5	
inmate	4		institute	18	4a
inmost	6		institution	14	4b
inn	21	3b	instruct	26	3a
inner	15	4b	instruction	26	3a
innkeeper	6		instructive	4	
innocence	14	4b	instructor	6	
innocent	26	3a	instrument	28	3a
innovation	4		insufficient	3	
innumerable	8		insulate	3	
inoffensive	3		insulator	3	
inquire	26	3a	insult	17	4a

inland 12 5a

insurance	10	5b	intricate	4	
insure	6		introduce	26	3a
insurgent	3		introduction	9	
insurrection	7		intrude	6	
integrity	7		intrust	6	
intellect	6		invade	17	4a
intellectual	6		invader	4	
intelligence	17	4a	invalid	6	
intelligent	11	5b	invariable	5	
intend	39	2a	invasion	7	
intense	9		invent	21	3b
intent	20	3b	invention	21	3b
intention	16	4a	inventor	8	
inter	5		invert	9	
intercept	6		invest	13	5a
intercession	4		investigate	9	
interchange	6		investigation	9	
intercourse	7		investment	5	
interest	68	1b	inveterate	4	
interfere	9		invigorate	4	
interior	19	3b	invincible	4	
internal	10	5b	invisible	15	4b
international	5		invitation	24	3a
internationalize	5		invite	44	2a
interpose	7		invoice	4	
interpret	10	5b	involuntary	6	
interpretation	6		involve	14	4b
interpreter	7		inward	16	4a
interrogative	3		iodine	3	
interrupt	20	3b	Iowa	7	
interruption	3		ire	4	
interval	13	5a	Ireland	11	
intervene	3		Irene	5	
interview	10	5b	iris	9	
intestine	4		Irish	15	4b
intimate	11	5b	Irishman	5	
into	163	1a1	irksome	4	
intolerable	4		iron	74	1b
intolerance	3		irregular	15	4b
intoxicate	5		irresistible	5	

irrigate	5		Jane	12	5a
irrigation	5		janitor	6	
irritable	3		January	36	2a
is	187	1a1	Japan	16	4a
Isaac	7		Japanese	12	5a
Isabel(le)	7		jar	25	3a
isinglass	3		jasper (J)	4	
island	66	1b	javelin	5	
islander	3		jaw	24	3a
isle	24	3a	jay (J)	8	
isn't	9		jealous	21	3b
Israel	16	4a	jealousy	17	4a
issue	38	2a	Jean	11	5b
isthmus	21	3b	jeer	5	
it	199	1a1	Jefferson	6	
Italian	28	3a	Jehovah	5	
Italy	28	3a	jelly	16	4a
itch	8		jeopardy	4	
item	14	4b	Jeremiah	4	
its	114	1a2	Jericho	4	
it's	15	4b	jerk	7	
itself	48	2a	jerkin	4	
I've	20	3b	Jerry	5	
ivory	22	3b	jersey (J)	16	4a
ivy	12	5a	Jesse	4	
			Jessie	3	
			jest	15	4b
			Jesu	4	
jack (J)	38	2a	Jesus	11	5b
jackal	4		jet	13	5a
jacket	13	5a	Jew	16	4a
Jackson	10	5b	jewel	28	3a
Jacob	18	4a	jeweler	3	
jade	3		jewelry	14	4b
jail	10	5b	Jewish	4	
jailor	4		jig	7	
jam	6		Jill	4	
James	42	2a	Jim	9	
Jamestown	9		jingle	6	
Jan.	10	5b	Jo	6	

Jerusalem 13 5a

Joan	5			Juliet	6	
job (J)	25	3a		Julius	6	
jockey	3			July	48	2a
jocund	8			jumble	3	
Joe	14	4b		jump	49	1b
Joel	3			junction	4	
jog	4			June	44	2a
John	77	1a5		jungle	4	
Johnny	12	5a		junior	12	5a
Johnson	8			juniper	5	
join	57	1b		junk	5	
joint	25	3a		Juno	5	
joke	21	3b		Jupiter	6	
jollity	3			jurisdiction	4	
jolly	16	4a		jury	9	
Jonathan	6			just	140	1a2
Jones	8			justice	43	2a
Jordan	7			justify	18	4a
Joseph	27	3a		jut	8	
Joshua	6					
jot	4					
journal	10	5b				
journey	51	1b		kangaroo	3	
Jove	10	5b		Kansas	8	
jovial	5			Kate	29	2b
joy	65	1b		Katherine	7	
joyful	29	2b		Katie	4	
joyless	3			keel	6	
joyous	12	5a		keen	20	3b
jubilant	3			keep	112	1a2
jubilee	8			keeper	17	4a
Judah	7			keg	3	
Judas	5			ken	4	
judge	56	1b		kennel	6	
judgment	35	2b		Kent	5	
judicious	3			Kentucky	5	
jug	7			kept	67	1b
juice	19	3b		kerchief	5	
juicy	6			kernel	6	
Julia	10	5b		kerosene	8	

kettle	25	3a	knighthood	6	
key	38	2a	knightly	4	
keyhole	3		knit	27	3a
khaki	3		knives	8	
kick	34	2b	knob	7	
kid	32	2b	knock	39	2a
kidney	7		knoll	8	
kill	81	1a5	knot	22	3b
kilo	3		know	171	1a1
kilogram	5		knowledge	45	2a
kilometer	7		known	80	1a5
kimono	4		knuckle	4	
kin	10	5b	kodak	5	
kind	118	1a2			
kindergarten	5				
kindle	16	4a	label	10	5b
kindly	36	2a	labor	57	1b
kindness	31	2b	laboratory	5	
kindred	16	4a	laborer	12	5a
kine	5		laborious	8	
king	99	1a3	labyrinth	5	
kingdom	39	2a	lace	32	2b
kingly	11	5b	lack	40	2a
kinsman	10	5b	lad	40	2a
kiss	52	1b	ladder	23	3a
kit	6		lade (n)	19	3b
kitchen	44	2a	ladies	29	2b
kite	14	4b	lading	5	
kitten	25	3a	ladle	6	
kitty (K)	15	4b	lady	63	1b
knave	17	4a	Lafayette	6	
knead	6		lag	10	5b
knee	52	1b	laid	58	1b
kneel	19	3b	lain	10	5b
knell	19	3b	lake	71	1b
knelt	6		lamb	39	2a
knew	67	1b	lambkin	5	
knickerbocker (K)	5		lame	27	3a
knife	45	2a	lament	16	4a
knight (K)	36	2a	lamentable	6	

lamentation	11	5b
lamp	47	2a
lance	16	4a
Lancelot	4	
land	122	1a2
landlord	4	
landmark	6	
landscape	12	5a
landward	3	
lane	25	3a
language	48	2a
languid	6	
languish	12	5a
lank	3	
lantern	14	4b
lap	34	2b
lapse	7	
lard	17	4a
large	123	1a2
lark	25	3a
La Salle	4	
lascivious	6	
lash	13	5a
lass	11	5b
last	149	1a2
latch	12	5a
late	98	1a3
lathe	4	
Latin	26	3a
latitude	7	
latter	32	2b
lattice	4	
laud	4	
laugh	78	1a5
laughter	28	3a
launch	13	5a
launder	3	
laundry	11	5b
Laura	4	
laurel	14	4b
lava	5	
lavatory	3	
lavish	11	5b
law	84	1a5
lawful	10	5b
lawgiver	3	
lawless	9	
lawmaker	5	
lawn	31	2b
Lawrence	9	
lawyer	21	3b
laxative	3	
lay	95	1a3
layer	13	5a
layette	4	
lazy	29	2b
lb.	14	4b
lea	8	
lead	80	1a5
leader	41	2a
leadership	6	
leaf	11	5b
leafless	6	
leafy	6	
league	35	2b
leak	8	
lean	37	2a
leap	44	2a
learn	103	1a3
lease	7	
least	59	1b
leather	42	2a
leathern	4	
leave	117	1a2
leaven	7	
leaves	4	
Lebanon	7	
lecture	14	4b
lecturer	4	
led	51	1b

ledge	10	5b	level	42	2a
lee(L)	14	4b	lever	3	
leek	4		Levi	5	
leer	4		Levite	5	
left	119	1a2	levy	9	
leg	65	1b	lewd	7	
legacy	5		lewdness	5	
legal	10	5b	Lewis	6	
legate	4		liable	9	
legend	10	5b	liar	13	5a
leggings	7		libel	4	
legible	3		liberal	19	3b
legion	14	4b	liberality	5	
legislate	3		liberty	45	2a
legislation	7		library	34	2b
legislative	4		lice	4	
legislature	11	5b	license	15	4b
legitimate	6		lick	18	4a
leisure	13	5a	lid	19	3b
lemon	18	4a	lie	74	1b
lemonade	12	5a	lief	5	
lend	28	3a	liege	7	
lender	4		lieutenant	14	4b
length	78	1a5	life	117	1a2
lengthen	9		lifeless	6	
lens	4		lifelong	4	
lent	14	4b	lifetime	6	
Leonard	9		lift	58	1b
leopard	5		lifter	3	
leper	5		light	120	1a2
leprosy	5		lighten	18	5a
less	84	1a5	lighthouse	8	
lessen	11	5b	lightness	3	
lesser	10	5b	lightning	24	3a
lesson	56	1b	lightship	3	
lest	26	3a	like	172	1a1
let	132	1a2	likely	25	3a
let's	8		liken	7	
letter	93	1a4	likeness	12	5a
lettuce	10	5b	likewise	15	4b

lilac	4		liver	15	4b
lily	28	3a	livery	11	5b
limb	31	2b	lizard	4	
lime	19	3b	lo	15	4b
limit	39	2a	load	50	1b
limp	10	5b	loaf	15	4b
Lincoln	21	3b	loam	4	
linden	7		loan	6	
line	97	1a3	loath	5	
lineal	4		loathe	10	5b
lineament	5		loathsome	7	
linen	30	2b	loaves	5	
linger	19	3b	lobster	4	
lingerie	4		local	25	3a
liniment	4		locality	5	
lining	12	5a	locate	23	3a
link	22	3b	location	14	4b
linoleum	5		lock	43	2a
linseed	5		locket	4	
lint	3		locomotive	10	5b
lion	52	1b	locust	9	
lioness	3		lodge	39	2a
lip	50	1b	lodging	8	
liquid	21	3b	loft	6	
liquor	16	4a	lofty	22	3b
lisle	3		log	35	2b
lisp	8		logic	6	
list	54	1b	loin	15	4b
listen	56	1b	Lois	6	
listener	5		loiter	9	
listerine	3		London	40	2a
listless	5		lone	27	3a
lit	9		loneliness	4	
literary	11	5b	lonely	16	4a
literature	15	4b	lonesome	12	5a
litter	11	5b	long	174	1a1
little	172	1a1	Longfellow	8	
live	139	1a2	longitude	6	
livelong	6		look	144	1a2
lively	27	3a	lookout	6	

loom	12	5a	lukewarm	3	
loop	14	4b	lull	16	4a
loose	47	2a	lullaby	6	
loosen	9		lumber	30	2b
lop	5		lumberman	4	
lord (L)	59	1b	luminous	7	
lordly	5		lump	15	4b
lordship	9		lunatic	5	
lore	4		lunch	21	3b
lose	63	1b	luncheon	9	
loser	5		lung	15	4b
loss	51	1b	lure	11	5b
lost	76	1a5	lurk	16	4a
lot	60	1b	lust	15	4b
lotus	5		luster	14	4b
loud	57	1b	lusty	11	5b
Louis	17	4a	lute	9	
Louisiana	5		Luther	5	
lounge	5		Lutheran	3	
lovable	4		luxuriant	5	
love	112	1a2	luxurious	7	
loveliness	3		luxury	23	3a
lovely	44	2a	lying	37	2a
lover	30	2b	Lynn	5	
low	91	1a4	Lyons	4	
lower	51	1b			
lowland	10	5b	ma	9	
lowliness	4		Mabel	8	
lowly	8		macaroon	3	
loyal	16	4a	Macedonia	5	
loyalty	10	5b	machine	42	2a
lubricant	3		machinery	22	3b
lubricate	3		machinist	4	
lubricator	4		mad	38	2a
lucid	4		madam	21	3b
luck	24	3a	madcap	3	
luckless	4		madden	5	
lucky	17	4a	made	107	1a3
Lucy	13	5a	Madeira	4	
Luke	4		Madison	14	4b

Lowell 6   luggage 8   lyre 8

madman	9	
madness	15	4b
Madonna	4	
madras (M)	5	
Madrid	5	
magazine	15	4b
Magdalen	5	
magic	25	3a
magical	3	
magician	6	
magistrate	14	4b
magnanimity	4	
magnanimous	3	
magnet	6	
magneto	4	
magnificence	9	
magnificent	23	3a
magnify	13	5a
magnitude	4	
magpie	6	
mahogany	8	
maid	40	2a
maiden	35	2b
maidenhood	3	
mail	49	1b
maim	7	
main	44	2a
Maine	8	
mainland	5	
maintain	31	2b
maintenance	5	
majestic	14	4b
majesty	22	3b
major	17	4a
majority	27	3a
make	176	1a1
maker	24	3a
malady	5	
male	21	3b
malice	13	5a
malicious	7	
mallet	5	
malt	5	
mama	6	
mamma	28	3a
mammy	3	
man	175	1a1
manage	29	2b
management	10	5b
manager	8	
Manasseh	4	
mane	12	5a
manful	4	
manger	11	5b
mangle	4	
Manhattan	12	5a
manhood	12	5a
manifest	16	4a
manifestation	3	
manifold	11	5b
Manila	5	
mankind	24	3a
manly	13	5a
manna	4	
manner	58	1b
mansion	18	4a
mantel	4	
mantle	22	3b
manual	5	
manufacture	29	2b
manufacturer	11	5b
manure	9	
manuscript	5	
many	153	1a1
map	47	2a
maple	16	4a
mar	12	5a
marble	35	2b
march (M)	74	1b
Marcus	4	

mare	14	4b	massy	8	
Margaret	16	4a	mast	23	3a
marge	4		master	74	1b
Margery	12	5a	masterpiece	6	
margin	13	5a	mastery	3	
Maria	7		mat	22	3b
Marian	4		match	41	2a
Marie	5		matchless	7	
marine	9		mate	30	2b
mariner	13	5a	material	45	2a
Marion	12	5a	maternal	6	
mark	90	1a4	maternity	3	
marker	3		mathematics	8	
market	61	1b	matin	4	
marketplace	4		matrimony	3	
marmalade	4		matron	10	5b
marriage	27	3a	matter	107	1a3
married	30	2b	Matthew	6	
marrow	6		mattock	5	
marry	37	2a	mattress	7	
Mars	6		mature	16	4a
marsh	12	5a	maturity	4	
marshal	12	5a	Maud	13	5a
marshy	4		maul	5	
mart	5		Max	5	
Martha	10	5b	maxim	7	
martial	9		maximum	4	
Martin	11	5b	may (M)	149	1a2
martyr	12	5a	maybe	18	4a
marvelous	21	3b	Mayflower	5	
Mary	48	2a	mayor	23	3a
Maryland	11	5b	mayst	9	
masculine	10	5b	maze	8	
mash	7		me	157	1a1
mask	15	4b	mead	12	5a
mason	13	5a	meadow	44	2a
mass	39	2a	meager (re)	6	
Massachusetts	15	4b	meal	45	2a
massacre	6		mean	100	1a3
massive	5		meant	36	2a

marvel 18 4a

meantime	15	4b		mention	43	2a
meanwhile	14	4b		meow	4	
measure	79	1a5		mercenary	5	
measurement	10	5b		mercerize	4	
meat	60	1b		merchandise	17	4a
mechanic	19	3b		merchant	39	2a
mechanical	5			merciful	9	
medal	11	5a		merciless	8	
meddle	13	5a		mercury	11	5b
mediator	4			mercy	35	2b
medical	10	5b		mere	40	2a
medicine	29	2b		meridian	8	
meditate	10	5b		merit	28	3a
meditation	8			Merlin	7	
meditative	4			mermaid	5	
Mediterranean	8			merriment	4	
medium	14	4b		merry	49	1b
medley	3			mesh	5	
meed	5			mess	10	5b
meek	17	4a		message	38	2a
meekness	8			messaline	4	
meet	104	1a3		messenger	24	3a
Meg	7			met	59	1b
melancholy	11	5b		metal	32	2b
mellow	13	5a		mete	4	
melodious	5			meteor	10	5b
melody	15	4b		meter(re)	16	4a
melon	9			methinks	11	5b
melt	45	2a		method	24	3a
member	52	1b		Methodist	3	
membership	7			methought	8	
memorable	4			metropolis	6	
memorial	16	4a		metropolitan	3	
memorize	7			mettle	4	
memory	43	2a		mew	18	4a
men	119	1a2		Mexican	8	
menace	4			Mexico	18	4a
menagerie	3			mi.	7	
mend	25	3a		mica	4	
mental	6			mice	18	4a

Michael	9			mine	77	1a5
Michigan	9			miner	8	
mid	16	4a		mineral	15	4b
midday	5			mingle	22	3b
middle	65	1b		miniature	5	
middy	4			minimum	5	
midnight	40	2a		minion	5	
midst	28	3a		minister	35	2b
midsummer	7			ministration	4	
midway	6			ministry	8	
midwinter	4			Minnesota	7	
mien	7			minnow	5	
might	107	1a3		minor	4	
mighty	49	1b		minority	4	
migration	4			minster	5	
Milan	5			minstrel	9	
milch	3			mint	9	
mild	30	2b		minus	4	
Mildred	4			minute	75	1b
mile	79	1a5		miracle	16	4a
military	25	3a		miraculous	4	
militia	7			mire	12	5a
milk	84	1a5		Miriam	5	
milkmaid	6			mirror	24	3a
milkman	3			mirth	20	3b
milkweed	4			miscarry	3	
milky	8			miscellaneous	3	
mill	57	1b		mischance	5	
miller	19	3b		mischief	22	3b
millinery	4			mischievous	5	
million	43	2a		misdemeanor	3	
millionaire	6			miser	8	
millstone	7			miserable	18	4a
Milton	10	5b		misery	20	3b
Milwaukee	4			misfortune	12	5a
mimic	6			misgiving	3	
min.	5			mishap	8	
mince	8			mislead	5	
mind	88	1a4		misled	3	
mindful	7			misplace	3	

miss (M)	83	1a5		moisture	14	4b
mission	12	5a		molasses	5	
missionary	8			mold	6	
Mississippi	21	3b		molder (*see* moulder)		
Missouri	10	5b		moldy (*see* mouldy)		
mist	26	3a		mole	13	5a
mistake	40	2a		molest	7	
mistletoe	3			Molly	8	
mistress	32	2b		molten	8	
mistrust	8			moment	71	1b
misty	9			momentary	4	
misunderstand	7			monarch	22	3b
misuse	5			monarchy	7	
Mitchell	6			monastery	3	
mite	3			Monday	38	2a
miter (re)	9			money	109	1a3
mitigate	5			monitor	4	
mitt	3			monk	13	5a
mitten	12	5a		monkey	19	4a
mix	45	2a		monotonous	3	
mixer	3			Monroe	7	
mixture	18	4a		Monsieur	4	
moan	19	3b		monster	15	4b
moat	6			monstrous	16	4a
mob	10	5b		Montana	3	
moccasin	7			month	82	1a5
mock	30	2b		monthly	9	
mocker	5			Montreal	5	
mockery	8			monument	25	3a
mode	22	3b		monumental	4	
model	30	2b		mood	16	4a
moderate	23	3a		moody	3	
modern	30	2b		moon	65	1b
modernize	3			moonbeam	4	
modest	24	3a		moonlight	15	4b
modesty	8			moonshine	4	
modify	3			moor (M)	19	3b
mohair	5			moorish (M)	3	
moist	16	4a		moorland	4	
moisten	8			mop	4	

mister   8

mope	3		mount	54	1b
moral	27	3a	mountain	77	1a5
moralist	3		mountaineer	5	
morality	5		mountainous	12	5a
moralize	3		mourn	29	2b
more	167	1a1	mourner	7	
moreover	22	3b	mournful	10	5b
morn	18	4a	mouse	38	2a
morning	102	1a3	mouth	69	1b
morris (M)	5		mouthful	4	
morrow	14	4b	movable	8	
Morse	5		move	84	1a5
morsel	10	5b	movement	25	3a
mortal	33	2b	mover	3	
mortality	5		mow	7	
mortar	4		mower	9	
mortgage	8		Mr.	63	1b
mortify	6		Mrs.	54	1b
Moscow	4		much	157	1a1
Moses	11	5b	muck	9	
mosquito	5		mud	34	2b
moss	20	3b	muddy	9	
mossy	7		muff	8	
most	125	1a2	muffin	6	
moth	11	5b	Muffit	5	
mother	109	1a3	muffle	6	
motion	29	2b	muffler	5	
motionless	6		mug	9	
motive	21	3b	mulberry	7	
motley	5		mule	17	4a
motor	16	4a	mull	4	
motorcycle	5		multiplication	8	
motorist	3		multiply	24	3a
motorman	4		multitude	20	3b
mottle	4		mum	3	
motto	7		munch	5	
mould	16	4a	Munich	5	
moulder	6		municipal	3	
mouldy	5		murder	28	3a
mound	14	4b	murderer	13	5a

murderous	5		nameless	8	
murmur	38	2a	namely	11	5b
muscle	9		Nan	5	
muscular	4		nap	15	4b
muse	22	3b	napkin	20	3b
museum	17	4a	Napoleon	4	
mush	3		narrate	3	
mushroom	5		narrative	7	
music	71	1b	narrow	57	1b
musical	23	3a	nasal	4	
musician	15	4b	Nat	7	
musk	5		Nathan	6	
musket	5		Nathaniel	6	
muskrat	4		nation	57	1b
muslin	8		national	35	2b
must	115	1a2	nationality	5	
mustard	7		native	45	2a
muster	9		nativity	6	
mute	19	3b	natural	50	1b
mutilate	3		nature	61	1b
mutinous	4		naught	10	5b
mutiny	6		naughty	15	4b
mutter	15	4b	naval	6	
mutton	11	5b	nave	4	
mutual	14	4b	navigable	8	
muzzle	11	5b	navigate	3	
my	152	1a1	navigation	6	
myriad	9		navigator	6	
myrrh	5		navy	23	3a
myrtle	9		nay	17	4a
myself	57	1b	Nazareth	3	
mysterious	15	4b	Nazarite	4	
mystery	24	3a	near	117	1a2
mystic	5		nearby	5	
			neat	27	3a
nag	3		neatness	3	
nail	42	2a	Nebraska	3	
naked	25	3a	necessary	57	1b
nakedness	7		necessity	27	3a
name	134	1a2	neck	58	1b

necklace	9		never	111	1a3
necktie	7		nevertheless	16	4a
neckwear	3		new	160	1a1
nectar	5		Newark	5	
Ned	15	4b	newborn	6	
need	109	1a3	newcomer	5	
needful	11	5b	Newfoundland	7	
needle	33	2b	Newport	5	
needless	11	5b	news	45	2a
needlewoman	5		newspaper	31	2b
needy	6		Newton	3	
ne'er	11	5b	New York	52	1b
negate	4		next	97	1a3
negative	9		Niagara	7	
neglect	32	2b	nibble	8	
negligence	4		nice	56	1b
negligent	4		Nicholas	8	
negotiate	5		nick	7	
negro	26	3a	nickel	15	4b
neigh	11	5b	nickname	4	
neighbor	66	1b	niece	8	
neighborhood	28	3a	nigh	16	4a
neither	57	1b	night	122	1a2
Nell	13		nightcap	3	
Nellie	3		nightgown	4	
Nelly	5		nightingale	15	4b
nephew	19	3b	nightly	9	
Neptune	4		nightmare	3	
nerve	16	4a	nightshirt	3	
nervous	15	4b	Nile	7	
nervousness	3		nimble	11	5b
nest	51	1b	nine	59	1b
nestle	9		nineteen	16	4a
net	36	2a	nineteenth	5	
nether	8		ninety	21	3b
Netherlands	11	5b	nip	10	5b
nettle	6		nipple	4	
network	4		no	181	1a1
neutral	3		no.	3	
neutrality	4		Noah	8	

ninth 24 3a

nobility	11	5b		notebook	4	
noble(ly)	46	2a		nothing	100	1a3
nobleman	8			notice	55	1b
nobleness	4			noticeable	5	
nobody	34	2b		notify	11	5b
nod	31	2b		notion	21	3b
noise	49	1b		notorious	5	
noiseless	9			Nottingham	5	
noisy	8			notwithstanding	10	5b
nomad	4			nought	13	5a
nominate	6			noun	3	
nomination	9			nourish	13	5a
none	58	1b		nourishment	8	
nonsense	13	5a		Nov.	6	
nook	10	5b		novel	13	5a
noon	58	1b		novelty	15	4b
noonday	11	5b		November	36	2a
noontide	7			novice	6	
noose	3			now	174	1a1
nor	73	1b		nowadays	6	
Norfolk	4			nowhere	9	
normal	13	5a		noxious	4	
Norman	6			nozzle	4	
Normandy	5			numb	3	
north	88	1a4		number	104	1a3
northeast	7			numberless	5	
northeastern	4			numeral	6	
northerly	4			numerous	27	3a
northern	34	2b		nun	11	5b
Northumberland	4			nunnery	4	
northward	3			nuptial	7	
northwest	12	5a		nurse	39	2a
northwestern	6			nursery	9	
Norway	10	5b		nut	47	2a
nose	50	1b		nutmeg	5	
nostril	16	4a		nutting	4	
not	203	1a1		nymph	12	5a
notable	13	5a				
notch	4			O	72	1b
note	65	1b		oak	51	1b

oaken	5		ocean	51	1b
Oakland	3		o'clock	45	3a
oakum	4		Oct.	7	
oar	15	4b	October	37	2a
oasis	7		odd	30	2b
oat	27	3a	ode	4	
oath	6		odious	9	
oatmeal	7		odor	22	3b
obedience	17	4a	odorous	4	
obedient	13	5a	o'er	28	3a
obey	47	2a	of	205	1a1
object	50	1b	off	105	1a3
objection	10	5b	offend	25	3a
obligation	10	5b	offender	8	
oblige	31	2b	offense	25	3a
oblique	3		offensive	6	
oblivion	6		offer	68	1b
obnoxious	3		office	69	1b
obscene	6		officer	53	1b
obscure	13	5a	official	28	3a
obscurity	6		officious	5	
obsequious	4		offspring	11	5b
observance	6		oft	22	3b
observation	17	4a	often	86	1a4
observe	42	2a	oftentimes	6	
observer	5		ofttimes	5	
obstacle	10	5b	ogre	5	
obstinate	10	5b	oh	67	1b
obstruct	5		Ohio	17	4a
obstruction	4		oil	49	2a
obtain	48	2a	oilcloth	5	
obtainable	4		oily	5	
obvious	6		ointment	8	
occasion	40	2a	Oklahoma	6	
occasional	14	4b	old	155	1a1
occidental	3		olden	4	
occupant	6		olfactory	3	
occupation	20	3b	olive	25	3a
occupy	38	2a	Oliver	12	5a
occur	29	2b	Olympus	4	

omen	5		orchard	30	2b
ominous	4		orchestra	11	5b
omit	14	4b	ordain	14	4b
omnipotent	5		ordeal	3	
on	200	1a1	order	100	1a3
once	111	1a3	ordinance	14	4b
one	199	1a1	ordinary	27	3a
oneself	4		ore	10	5b
onion	19	3b	Oregon	8	
only	156	1a1	organ	29	2b
onset	4		organist	6	
onward	22	3b	organization	11	5b
onyx	3		organize	15	4b
ooze	3		orient (O)	13	5a
open	126	1a2	oriental (O)	8	
opera	18	4a	origin	13	5a
operate	10	5b	original	24	3a
operation	29	2b	originate	5	
opinion	37	2a	oriole	6	
opponent	7		Orleans	9	
opportune	5		ornament	27	3a
opportunity	32	2b	orphan	16	4a
oppose	25	3a	ostrich	9	
opposite	34	2b	other	168	1a1
opposition	15	5a	otherwise	27	3a
oppress	18	4a	ought	49	1b
oppression	12	5a	ounce	23	3a
oppressive	3		our	172	1a1
oppressor	5		ours	23	3a
optic	3		ourself	20	3b
optical	3		ourselves	26	3a
or	181	1a1	out	193	1a1
oracle	12	5a	outbreak	5	
oral	6		outcast	5	
orange	44	2a	outcry	4	
oration	8		outdoor(s)	8	
orator	9		outer	9	
oratory	3		outfit	9	
orb	12	5a	outgo	5	
orbit	4		outing	6	

Outlandish to Painful

outlandish	4		overseer	3	
outlaw	4		overshadow	3	
outlet	14	4b	overshoe	6	
outline	13	5a	oversight	5	
outlive	5		overspread	6	
outlook	3		overtake	17	4a
outlying	3		overthrew	6	
outrage	8		overthrow	17	4a
outrageous	3		overtook	8	
outright	3		overturn	13	5a
outrun	9		overwhelm	10	5b
outside	50	1b	owe	46	2a
outspread	6		owl	33	2b
outstretch	8		owlet	5	
outstrip	4		own	117	1a2
outward	19	3b	owner	36	2b
oval	4		ownership	4	
oven	22	3b	ox(oxen)	36	2b
over	168	1a1	Oxford	12	5a
overalls	6		oyster	16	4a
overbear	3		oz.	14	4b
overboard	4				
overcame	7		pa	10	5b
overcast	5		pace	31	2b
overcoat	14	4b	pacific (P)	21	3b
overcome	22	3b	pacify	3	
overflow	18	4a	pack	38	2a
overgrow (n)	4		package	28	3a
overhang	3		packer	3	
overhead	14	4b	packet	6	
overhear	7		pad	12	5a
overjoy	3		paddle	10	5b
overlaid	3		padlock	3	
overland	5		pagan	5	
overlay	4		page	65	1b
overleap	3		pageant	7	
overlook	14	4b	paid	37	2a
overpower	5		pail	25	3a
overrun	5		pain	54	1b
oversea (s)	4		painful	12	5a

paint	51	1b	parch	10	5b
painter	21	3b	parchment	6	
pair	60	1b	pardon	33	2b
pajama (s)	5		pare	8	
pal	4		parent	41	2a
palace	41	2a	parentage	3	
palate	3		Paris	19	3b
pale	35	2b	parish	9	
paleface (d)	4		Parisian	5	
Palestine	6		park	42	2a
palfrey	4		parley	4	
pall	6		parliament	17	4a
palm	26	3a	parliamentary	3	
palpable	3		parlor	26	3a
palsy	6		parrot	11	5b
pamper	3		parsley	5	
pamphlet	5		parson	14	4b
pan (P)	34	2b	part	145	1a2
Panama	15	4b	partake	11	5b
pancake	10	5b	partaker	5	
Pandora	4		partial	10	5b
pane	15	4b	participate	7	
panel	3		particle	8	
pang	16	4a	particular	37	2a
panic	5		partition	6	
pansy (P)	12	5a	partly	29	2b
pant	23	3a	partner	20	3b
pantaloon	6		partridge	10	5b
pantry	12	5a	party	65	1b
papa	25	3a	pass	112	1a2
paper	92	1a4	passage	25	3a
parable	4		passenger	28	3a
parade	12	5a	passion	27	3a
paradise	24	3a	passionate	8	
paraffin	4		passive	5	
paragraph	8		past	75	1b
parallel	15	4b	paste	10	5b
paramour	5		pastime	14	4b
parasol	3		pastor	12	5a
parcel	26	3a	pastoral	5	

pastry	6			pebble	13	5a
pasture	31	2b		pecan	3	
pat	22	3b		peck	20	3b
patch	26	3a		peculiar	23	3a
patent	12	5a		peculiarity	5	
paternal	7			pedal	4	
path	52	1b		pedant	3	
pathetic	4			peddler	7	
pathway	10	5b		pedestal	6	
patience	23	3a		pedigree	3	
patient	36	2b		peek	4	
Patrick	4			peel	12	5a
patriot	10	5b		peep	29	2b
patriotic	9			peer	30	2b
patron	16	4a		peerless	5	
patter	7			peevish	4	
pattern	29	2b		peg	12	5a
patty	6			pelt	5	
Paul	23	3a		pen	51	1b
pause	22	3b		penalty	5	
pave	15	4b		penance	7	
pavement	14	4b		pence	7	
pavilion	8			pencil	34	2b
paw	23	3a		pendant	7	
pawn	4			pendent	5	
pay	93	1a4		pending	3	
payable	5			penetrate	7	
payment	23	3a		peninsula	13	5a
pea	25	3a		penitent	7	
peace	64	1b		Penn	6	
peaceable	8			Pennsylvania	19	3b
peaceful	21	3b		penny	35	2b
peach	24	3a		pension	9	
peacock	12	5a		pensive	13	5a
peak	15	4b		pent	7	
peal	14	4b		pentagon	3	
peanut	7			penury	6	
pear	23	3a		people	126	1a2
pearl	36	2b		pepper	16	4a
peasant	19	3b		pepsin	3	

per	31	2b		perseverance	7	
peradventure	7			persevere	7	
percale	4			Persia (n)	12	5a
perceive	24	3a		persist	9	
percent	7			person	76	1a5
percentage	3			personage	6	
perception	5			personal	19	3b
perch	21	3b		personality	5	
perchance	11	5b		perspective	3	
percolate	3			perspiration	4	
perdition	6			persuade	22	3b
perennial	3			persuasion	6	
perfect	62	1b		pert	5	
perfection	14	4b		pertain	8	
perform	34	2b		Peru	9	
performance	13	5a		peruse	7	
performer	3			pervade	6	
perfume	19	3b		perverse	7	
perhaps	62	1b		pervert	6	
peril	14	4b		pest	4	
perilous	12	5a		pestilence	9	
period	34	2b		pet	17	4a
periodical	9			petal	8	
perish	27	3a		Peter	35	2b
perjure	4			petition	13	5a
perjury	3			petrify	3	
permanent	18	4a		petroleum	8	
permission	14	4b		petticoat	10	5b
permit	38	2a		petty	13	5a
pernicious	6			pew	6	
peroxide	3			phantom	9	
perpendicular	5			Pharisee	4	
perpetual	16	4a		Pharoah	6	
perpetuate	4			phase	3	
perplex	15	4b		pheasant	4	
perplexity	4			Philadelphia	19	3b
Perry	7			Philip	26	3a
persecute	11	5b		Philippine	8	
persecution	9			philistine (P)	10	5b
persecutor	3			philosopher	15	4b

philosophic	4			pillar	17	4a
philosophical	5			pillow	28	3a
philosophy	18	4a		pilot	10	5b
Phoebus	7			pin	37	2a
phoenix	3			pincers	4	
phone	12	5a		pinch	17	4a
phosphate	7			pine	35	2b
phosphorous	5			pineapple	6	
photo	5			pinion	6	
photograph	8			pink	29	2b
photographer	3			pinnace	4	
phrase	19	3b		pinnacle	6	
physic(s)	7			pint	17	4a
physical	10	5b		pioneer	11	5b
physician	24	3a		pious	16	4a
piano	17	4a		pipe	48	2a
piazza	6			piper	9	
pick	53	1b		pique	6	
picker	3			pirate	10	5b
pickerel	3			pistol	19	3b
picket	3			piston	4	
pickle	11	5b		pit	23	3a
picnic	15	4b		pitch	27	3a
picture	80	1a5		pitcher	19	3b
picturesque	10	5b		piteous	6	
pie	37	2a		pitiable	3	
piece	91	1a4		pitiful	9	
pier	9			pitiless	9	
pierce	21	3b		Pittsburgh	9	
piety	10	5b		pity	49	2a
pig	39	2a		pk.	7	
pigeon	15	4b		place	156	1a1
piggy	5			placid	5	
pike	7			plague	22	3b
Pilate	4			plaid	7	
pile	44	2a		plain	78	1a5
pilgrim	18	4a		plainness	4	
pilgrimage	8			plaint	3	
pill	13	5a		plaintive	5	
pillage	5			plait	5	

plan	72	1b		plow	27	3a
plane	15	4b		plowman	3	
planet	14	4b		pluck	29	2b
plank	13	5a		plug	7	
plant	95	1a3		plum	25	3a
Plantagenet	3			plumage	4	
plantation	13	5a		plumb	3	
planter	10	5b		plumber	4	
plaster	10	5b		plume	17	4a
plate	46	2a		plummet	3	
plateau	12	5a		plump	12	5a
platform	17	4a		plunder	12	5a
platinum	3			plunge	28	3a
Plato	5			pluperfect	4	
platter	10	5b		plus	6	
play	103	1a3		plush	4	
player	10	5b		ply	13	5a
playfellow	4			Plymouth	5	
playful	5			pneumatic	3	
playground	10	5b		pneumonia	4	
playhouse	4			pocket	47	2a
playmate	14	4b		pocketbook	3	
plaything	13	5a		pod	5	
plea	8			poem	27	3a
plead	22	3b		poet	37	2a
pleasant	64	1b		poetic	9	
pleasantness	3			poetical	4	
pleasantry	3			poetry	16	4a
please	93	1a4		point	105	1a3
pleasure	65	1b		poise	9	
pledge	21	3b		poison	25	3a
plenteous	8			poisonous	7	
plentiful	12	5a		poke	6	
plenty	43	2a		Poland	8	
pliers	3			polar	8	
plight	11	5b		pole (P)	47	2a
plod	5			police	17	4a
plot	25	3a		policeman	11	5b
plough	16	4a		policy	22	3b
ploughshare	3			polish (P)	22	3b

polite	22	3b		portal	8	
politeness	5			portentous	4	
politic	17	4a		porter	14	4b
political	18	4a		portière	6	
politician	5			portion	29	2b
politics	3			portrait	4	
poll	15	4b		portray	4	
pollen	4			Portugal	9	
pollute	7			Portuguese	8	
Polly	8			pose	5	
polo	6			position	28	3a
pomegranate	3			positive	13	5a
pomp	16	4a		possess	38	2a
Pompey	7			possession	36	2b
pompous	5			possessive	5	
pond	33	2b		possessor	3	
ponder	8			possibility	11	5b
ponderous	7			possible	59	1b
pongee	4			post	55	1b
pony	26	3a		postage	14	4b
pooh	3			postal	11	5b
pool	22	3b		postcard	4	
poor	101	1a3		posterity	10	5b
pop	11	5b		postman	7	
pope	20	3b		postmaster	3	
poplar	7			postoffice	11	5b
poplin	5			postpone	4	
poppy	10	5b		postscript	8	
populace	5			posture	4	
popular	22	3b		posy	4	
popularity	3			pot	39	2a
population	25	3a		potash	3	
populous	5			potato	38	2a
porcelain	7			potent	8	
porch	30	2b		potentate	7	
pore	9			potion	4	
pork	17	4a		Potomac	5	
porridge	5			potter	6	
port	38	2a		pouch	9	
portable	4			poultry	19	3b

pounce	5		prelate	7	
pound	60	1b	preliminary	8	
pour	45	2a	premature	4	
poverty	21	3b	premier	4	
powder	28	3a	premium	7	
power	85	1a4	prepaid	5	
powerful	22	3b	preparation	22	3b
powerless	5		preparatory	4	
practical	23	3a	prepare	57	1b
practice	50	1b	preposition	4	
prairie	11	5b	prerogative	5	
praise	44	2a	presage	5	
prance	7		presbyterian (P)	4	
prank	10	5b	prescribe	16	4a
prate	7		prescription	4	
prattle	5		presence	40	2a
pray	45	2a	present	102	1a3
prayer	40	2a	presentation	5	
preach	29	2b	presently	7	
preacher	13	5a	preservation	4	
precaution	3		preservative	3	
precede	9		preserve	37	2a
precedent	6		preserver	5	
precept	10	5b	preside	10	5b
precinct	7		presidency	4	
precious	36	2b	president	45	2a
precipice	7		presidential	5	
precise	9		press	55	1b
precocious	5		pressure	12	5a
predecessor	5		presume	19	3b
predict	7		presumption	5	
prediction	6		presumptuous	9	
predominant	3		pretend	21	3b
predominate	3		pretense (ce)	11	5b
preëminence	4		pretext	3	
prefer	41	2a	pretty	81	1a5
preference	5		prevail	24	3a
preferment	4		prevent	42	2a
pregnant	7		previous	16	4a
prejudice	9		prey	23	3a

price	59	1b	product	33	2b
prick	19	3b	production	12	5a
prickly	3		Prof.	4	
pride	42	2a	profane	10	5b
priest	28	3a	profess	12	5a
priesthood	4		profession	12	5a
primary	10	5b	professional	6	
prime	16	4a	professor	23	3a
primer	6		proffer	5	
primitive	4		proficient	3	
primrose	6		profile	3	
prince	55	1b	profit	34	2b
princely	6		profitable	12	5a
princess	27	3a	profound	13	5a
principal	36	2b	profuse	6	
principality	5		progeny	6	
principle	21	3b	program	11	5b
print	49	2a	progress	28	3a
printer	5		progressive	9	
prior	7		prohibit	13	5a
prison	34	2b	prohibition	5	
prisoner	38	2a	project	13	5a
privacy	4		prologue	4	
private	41	2a	prolong	17	4a
privilege	20	3b	promenade	7	
privy	8		prominent	16	4a
prize	36	2b	promise	65	1b
probability	5		promontory	4	
probable	36	2b	promote	9	
problem	23	3a	promotion	8	
proceed	38	2a	prompt	29	2b
process	23	3a	prone	6	
procession	15	4b	pronoun	7	
proclaim	24	3a	pronounce	33	2b
proclamation	7		pronunciation	7	
procure	17	4a	proof	32	2b
prodigal	6		prop	9	
prodigious	6		propagate	8	
prodigy	3		propensity	4	
produce	43	2a	proper	51	1b

property	36	2b	prudent	12	5a
prophecy	13	5a	prune	14	4b
prophesy	12	5a	Prussia	5	
prophet	24	3a	pry	5	
prophetic	7		psalm	10	5b
propitious	6		pt.	9	
proportion	23	3a	public	58	1b
proposal	7		publican	5	
propose	26	3a	publication	8	
proposition	10	5b	publish	28	3a
proprietor	7		publisher	7	
propriety	3		pudding	22	3b
prose	8		puddle	4	
prosecute	5		puff	24	3a
prosecution	3		pug	3	
prospect	24	3a	pull	58	1b
prospective	4		puller	7	
prosper	19	3b	pulley	3	
prosperity	14	4b	pulp	6	
prosperous	22	3b	pulpit	8	
prostrate	8		pulse	16	4a
protect	41	2a	pumice	3	
protection	21	3b	pump	23	3a
protector	9		pumpkin	14	4b
protest	15	4b	punch	11	5b
protestant (P)	7		punctual	9	
proud	62	1b	punish	33	2b
prove	63	1b	punishment	24	3a
proverb	9		puny	4	
provide	47	2a	pup	5	
providence	18	4a	pupil	39	2a
province	30	2b	puppet	3	
provision	19	3b	puppy	11	5b
provocation	6		purchase	41	2a
provoke	22	3b	purchaser	4	
prow	4		pure	53	1b
prowess	8		pureness	4	
prowl	4		purge	10	5b
proximity	3		purify	9	
prudence	8		Puritan	8	

purity	13	5a	quick	87	1a4
purple	33	2b	quicken	16	4a
purpose	54	1b	quickness	3	
purr	6		quiet	62	1b
purse	34	2b	quietness	6	
pursue	33	2b	quietude	4	
pursuer	3		quill	5	
pursuit	14	4b	quilt	12	5a
push	40	2a	quince	3	
puss	8		quinine	6	
pussy	21	3b	quire	5	
put	131	1a2	quit	32	2b
putty	5		quite	73	1b
puzzle	14	4b	quiver	16	4a
pyramid	7		quotation	6	
Pyrrhus	3		quote	12	5a
			quoth	11	5b
qt.	12	5a	quotient	6	
quack	12	5a			
quail	9		rabbit	31	2b
quaint	13	5a	race	56	1b
quake	10	5b	racer	3	
quaker (Q)	5		Rachel	4	
qualification	3		rack	25	3a
qualify	6		racket	3	
quality	38	2a	radiant	12	5a
quantity	41	2a	radiator	8	
quarrel	34	2b	radical	5	
quarrelsome	5		radio	3	
quarry	12	5a	radish	4	
quart	19	3b	radius	5	
quarter	60	1b	raft	6	
Quebec	5		rafter	8	
queen	74	1b	rag	24	3a
queer	21	3b	rage	28	3a
quell	8		ragged	15	4b
quench	19	3b	raid	6	
query	4		rail	29	2b
quest	11	5b	railroad	42	2a
question	74	1b	railway	21	3b

raiment	7			rather	59	1b
rain	83	1a5		ratify	4	
rainbow	21	3b		rational	4	
raindrop	7			rattle	21	3b
rainfall	10	5b		rattlesnake	3	
rainy	18	4a		ravage	5	
raise	81	1a5		rave	12	5a
raiser	6			raven	22	3b
raisin	11	5b		ravenous	5	
rake	16	4a		ravine	3	
Raleigh	6			ravish	7	
rally	6			raw	26	3a
Ralph	20	3b		ray	35	2b
ram	18	4a		raze	6	
ramble	5			razor	9	
rampant	4			reach	93	1a4
rampart	5			reaction	3	
ran	56	1b		read	109	1a3
ranch	7			reader	16	4a
random	12	5a		readily	15	4b
rang	18	4a		readiness	7	
range	42	2a		ready	82	1a5
rank	39	2a		real	54	1b
ransom	11	5b		reality	10	5b
rap	13	5a		realize	20	3b
rape	5			really	36	2b
Raphael	4			realm	25	3a
rapid	53	1b		reap	21	3b
rapine	7			reaper	6	
rapt	8			reappear	5	
rapture	15	4b		rear	32	2b
rare	34	2b		reason	81	1a5
rarity	3			reasonable	16	4a
rascal	12	5a		rebel	21	3b
rascally	3			rebellion	11	5b
rash	14	4b		rebellious	9	
rashness	3			rebound	3	
raspberry	4			rebuild	7	
rat	32	2b		rebuke	11	5b
rate	46	2a		recall	20	3b

recapture	3		redden	7	
recede	3		reddish	5	
receipt	20	3b	redeem	14	4b
receive	88	1a4	redeemer	4	
receiver	6		redemption	6	
recent	26	3a	redouble	4	
receptacle	7		redoubt	4	
reception	13	5a	redress	8	
recess	19	3b	reduce	28	3a
recessive	5		reduction	10	5b
recipe	5		reed	21	3b
recital	3		reef	7	
recite	14	4b	reek	4	
reck	4		reel	19	3b
reckless	4		reëlect	3	
reckon	18	4a	reëlection	3	
reclaim	5		reënter	4	
recline	7		reëstablish	4	
recognition	6		refer	22	3b
recognize	25	3a	reference	12	5a
recoil	8		refine	19	3b
recollect	9		refinement	6	
recollection	5		reflect	18	4a
recommend	20	3b	reflection	13	5a
recommendation	11	5b	reflexive	4	
recompense	14	4b	reform	15	4b
reconcile	16	4a	reformation	4	
reconciliation	4		refrain	12	5a
record	44	2a	refresh	12	5a
recorder	3		refreshment	11	5b
recount	8		refrigerator	4	
recover	29	2b	refuge	19	3b
recovery	5		refund	3	
recreation	6		refusal	3	
recruit	6		refuse	44	2a
rectangle	11	5b	refute	7	
rectangular	6		regain	15	4b
rector	3		regal	11	5b
red	93	1a4	regard	42	2a
redbreast	7		regarding	5	

regardless	7		remain	80	1a5
regent	6		remainder	20	3b
regime	4		remark	20	3b
regiment	8		remarkable	20	3b
region	45	2a	remedy	27	3a
register	25	3a	remember	83	1a5
registration	6		remembrance	14	4b
regret	21	3b	remind	17	4a
regular	46	2a	reminder	3	
regulate	13	5a	remission	4	
regulation	9		remit	10	5b
rehearse	8		remittance	6	
reign	31	2b	remnant	14	4b
rein	19	3b	remonstrate	3	
reindeer	11	5b	remorse	10	5b
reiterate	6		remote	14	4b
reject	14	4b	removal	6	
rejoice	37	2a	remove	44	2a
relapse	3		remover	4	
relate	24	3a	rend	14	4b
relation	26	3a	render	29	2b
relationship	4		renew	26	3a
relative	23	3a	renewal	4	
relax	5		renounce	12	5a
relay	4		renown	20	3b
release	19	3b	rent	37	2a
relent	8		renter	4	
reliability	4		reopen	4	
reliable	8		reorganize	3	
reliance	3		repaid	4	
relic	11	5b	repair	39	2a
relief	27	3a	repairer	5	
relieve	25	3a	repast	5	
religion	24	3a	repay	14	4b
religious	26	3a	repeal	6	
relinquish	5		repeat	47	2a
relish	8		repel	7	
reluctance	3		repent	19	3b
reluctant	6		repentance	8	
rely	9		repetition	6	

repine	7		resistance	7	
replace	11	5b	resistless	3	
replenish	7		resolute	14	4b
reply	64	1b	resolution	13	5a
report	52	1b	resolve	26	3a
repose	22	3b	resort	20	3b
represent	40	2a	resound	13	5a
representation	10	5b	resource	9	
representative	24	3a	respect	38	2a
repress	3		respectable	5	
reproach	20	3b	respectful	10	5b
reprobate	4		respective	12	5a
reproof	9		respite	7	
reprove	10	5b	resplendent	7	
reptile	5		respond	13	5a
republic	21	3b	response	10	5b
republican	14	4b	responsibility	5	
repulse	5		responsible	9	
reputation	15	4b	rest	111	1a3
repute	8		restaurant	14	4b
request	34	2b	restful	3	
require	53	1b	restitution	4	
requirement	7		restless	21	3b
requite	7		restore	29	2b
rescue	22	3b	restorer	3	
research	4		restrain	19	3b
resemblance	5		restraint	13	5a
resemble	17	4a	restrict	3	
resent	5		result	48	2a
resentment	5		resume	17	4a
reservation	7		resurrection	4	
reserve	23	3a	retail	9	
reservoir	3		retain	19	3b
reside	18	4a	retinue	4	
residence	20	3b	retire	33	2b
resident	10	5b	retirement	6	
residue	4		retort	3	
resign	20	3b	retouch	3	
resignation	5		retrace	5	
resist	16	4a	retreat	20	3b

return	68	1b	Richard	16	4a
Reuben	7		riches	18	4a
reunion	3		Richmond	11	5b
reunite	4		richness	3	
Rev.	6		Rico	7	
reveal	23	3a	rid	25	3a
revel	13	5a	ridden	5	
revelation	6		riddle	16	4a
revenge	23	3a	ride	81	1a5
revenue	11	5b	rider	17	4a
reverberate	3		ridge	24	3a
revere	7		ridicule	4	
reverence	18	4a	ridiculous	8	
reverend	15	4b	rife	3	
reverent	7		rifle	10	5b
reverie (*see* revery)			rift	5	
reverse	15	4b	rig	10	5b
revert	3		right	120	1a2
revery	5		righteous	13	5a
review	32	2b	righteousness	9	
revile	7		rightful	6	
revive	14	4b	rigid	5	
revolt	15	4b	rigor	8	
revolution	18	4a	rigorous	3	
revolutionary	7		rill	16	4a
revolve	12	5a	rim	11	5b
revolver	4		rind	6	
reward	28	3a	ring	69	1b
Reynard	8		ringer	4	
rhetoric	4		ringlet	5	
rheumatism	7		rinse	4	
Rhine	12	5a	riot	14	4b
Rhode Island	5		riotous	5	
Rhone	4		rip	21	3b
rhyme	21	3b	ripe	33	2b
rib	25	3a	ripen	17	4a
ribband	6		ripple	12	5a
ribbon	33	2b	rise	72	1b
rice	23	3a	risen	6	
rich	90	1a4	risk	16	4a

rite	11	5b	Romeo	6	
rival	22	3b	romp	5	
river	101	1a3	romper	4	
riverside	7		rood	4	
rivet	6		roof	52	1b
rivulet	8		roofing	5	
roach	3		rook	7	
road	89	1a4	room	98	1a3
roadside	7		roomy	3	
roadway	4		Roosevelt	5	
roam	21	3b	rooster	11	5b
roar	42	2a	root	46	2a
roast	29	2b	rope	36	2b
roaster	3		Rosalind	4	
rob (R)	30	2b	Rosamund	6	
robber	25	3a	rose (R)	75	1b
robbery	8		rosebud	7	
robe	28	3a	rosette	3	
Robert	30	2b	rosin	4	
robin	33	2b	rosy	17	4a
Robinson	9		rot	10	5b
robust	3		rotary	7	
Rochester	5		rotten	12	5a
rock	85	1a4	rottenness	3	
rocker	3		rough	48	2a
rocket	3		round	105	1a3
rocky	18	4a	rouse	16	4a
rod	38	2a	rout	8	
rode	34	2b	route	26	3a
roe	8		rove	16	4a
Roger	10	5b	rover	13	5a
rogue	13	5a	row	54	1b
Roland	7		rowboat	3	
rôle	4		rower	3	
roll	80	1a5	Roy	5	
roller	12	5a	royal	39	2a
Roman	37	2a	royalty	6	
romance	8		rub	33	2b
romantic	8		rubber	24	3a
Rome	34	2b	rubbish	7	

ruby	10	5b
rudder	3	
ruddy	8	
rude	29	2b
rudeness	3	
rue	8	
ruffian	8	
ruffle	13	5a
Rufus	4	
rug	26	3a
rugged	13	5a
ruin	43	2a
ruinous	5	
rule	75	1b
ruler	28	3a
rum	4	
rumble	7	
ruminate	4	
rumor	15	4b
rump	7	
rumple	4	
run	115	1a2
runabout	3	
runaway	6	
rung	9	
runner	13	5a
rural	19	3b
rush	57	1b
Russell	4	
russet	6	
Russia (n)	26	3a
rust	19	3b
rustic	14	4b
rustle	15	4b
rusty	11	5b
Ruth	22	3b
ruthless	5	
rye	14	4b
Sabbath	17	4a

saber (re)	4	
sable	10	5b
sachet	4	
sack	29	2b
Sacramento	3	
sacred	24	3a
sacrifice	29	2b
sad	61	1b
sadden	5	
saddle	32	2b
Sadie	4	
sadness	14	4b
safe	60	1b
safeguard	5	
safety	33	2b
sage	16	4a
Sahara	3	
said	115	1a2
sail	82	1a5
sailboat	3	
sailor	36	2b
saint	36	2b
saintly	4	
saith	7	
sake	34	2b
salad	11	5b
salary	23	3a
sale	34	2b
Salem	4	
salesman	9	
Salisbury	5	
sally (S)	13	5a
salmon	9	
saloon	3	
salt	53	1b
salutary	4	
salutation	6	
salute	17	4a
salvation	11	5b
salve	3	

Sam	8			Saturday	31	2b
Samaria	4			Saturn	4	
same	129	1a2		satyr	6	
sample	16	4a		sauce	17	4a
Samson	7			saucepan	7	
Samuel	13	5a		saucer	9	
sanctify	10	5b		saucy	9	
sanction	6			Saul	8	
sanctity	6			saunter	4	
sanctuary	13	5a		sausage	10	5b
sand	53	1b		savage	30	2b
sandal	7			Savannah	4	
San Diego	4			save	84	1a5
sandman	4			saver	4	
sandpiper	5			savior (S)	12	5a
sandwich	11	5b		savor	8	
sandy	21	3b		savory	8	
sane	4			saw	102	1a3
San Francisco	11	5b		sawmill	4	
sang	34	2b		Saxon	6	
sanitary	9			say	140	1a2
sank	17	4a		scab	4	
Santa Claus	18	4a		scabbard	5	
Santa Fé	4			scaffold	7	
sap	18	4a		scald	5	
sapphire	6			scale	46	2a
Sara (h)	8			scallop	4	
sardine	4			scalp	11	5b
sarsaparilla	3			scaly	3	
sash	16	4a		scamper	8	
sat	59	1b		scan	8	
Sat.	3			scandal	9	
Satan	14	4b		scant	8	
sateen	4			scanty	11	5b
satiate	5			'scape	4	
satin	15	4b		scar	14	4b
satire	7			scarce	48	2a
satisfaction	19	3b		scare	25	3a
satisfactory	11	5b		scarecrow	3	
satisfy	41	2a		scarf	17	4a

scarlet	21	3b	scrap	15	4b
scatter	39	2a	scrape	20	3b
scene	34	2b	scraper	6	
scenery	7		scratch	25	3a
scenic	4		scrawl	5	
scent	15	4b	scream	23	3a
scepter (re)	15	4b	screech	6	
schedule	9		screen	17	4a
scheme	16	4a	screw	13	5a
scholar	18	4a	scribble	5	
scholarship	3		scribe	5	
school	104	1a3	scrim	4	
schoolboy	8		scripture	11	5b
schoolhouse	19	3b	scroll	9	
schoolmaster	10	5b	Scrooge	6	
schoolroom	13	5a	scrub	12	5a
science	23	3a	scruple	9	
scientific	4		scullion	4	
scissors	13	5a	sculptor	4	
scoff	11	5b	sculpture	7	
scold	21	3b	scum	4	
scoop	8		scurry	4	
scope	7		scythe	6	
scorch	10	5b	sea	100	1a3
score	32	2b	seacoast	8	
scorn	28	3a	seafaring	4	
scorner	5		seal	36	2b
scornful	10	5b	seam	14	4b
scorpion	5		seamen	11	5b
Scot	12	5a	seaport	9	
scotch (S)	14	4b	search	44	2a
Scotland	15	4b	seashore	5	
Scott	6		seasick	4	
Scottish	5		seaside	6	
scoundrel	5		season	61	1b
scour	13	5a	seasonable	3	
scourge	15	4b	seat	71	1b
scout	14	4b	seaward	6	
scowl	5		seclude	3	
scramble	10	5b	second	92	1a4

secondary	7			sensation	7	
secrecy	5			sensational	3	
secret	47	2a		sense	41	2a
secretary	22	3b		senseless	8	
sect	9			sensibility	3	
section	36	2b		sensible	14	4b
secure	46	2a		sensitive	5	
security	10	5b		sensual	5	
sedan	3			sent	84	1a5
sedate	3			sentence	27	3a
sediment	3			sentiment	10	5b
sedition	3			sentimental	3	
seduce	9			sentinel	4	
see	172	1a1		separate	50	1b
seed	63	1b		separation	12	5a
seek	59	1b		separator	4	
seem	100	1a3		Sept.	4	
seemingly	3			September	48	2a
seemly	3			sepulcher (re)	9	
seen	89	1a4		sequel	4	
seer	6			sequester (ed)	9	
seethe	6			seraph	4	
Seine	4			seraphim	4	
seize	50	1b		Serbia (n)	4	
seizure	4			serene	12	5a
seldom	34	2b		serge	6	
select	33	2b		sergeant	6	
selection	9			serial	3	
self	51	1b		series	15	4b
selfish	16	4a		serious	29	2b
selfishness	5			seriousness	3	
selfsame	12	5a		sermon	12	5a
sell	68	1b		serpent	18	4a
seller	5			servant	47	2a
selves	4			serve	77	1a5
semblance	7			server	5	
senate	23	3a		Servia (n) (*see* Serbia)		
senator	16	4a		service	67	1b
send	95	1a3		serviceable	3	
senior	9			servile	10	5b

servitude	7	
session	9	
set	110	1a3
settee	4	
settle	57	1b
settlement	27	3a
settler	18	4a
seven	73	1b
seventeen	14	4b
seventeenth	5	
seventh	25	3a
seventy	40	2a
sever	10	5b
several	81	1a5
severe	30	2b
severity	6	
sew	43	2a
sewer	7	
sex	15	4b
sexton	5	
shabby	4	
shade	51	1b
shadow	47	2a
shadowy	8	
shady	16	4a
shaft	18	4a
shaggy	7	
shake	50	1b
shaker	4	
Shakespeare	8	
shall	116	1a2
shallow	21	3b
shalt	23	3a
sham	5	
shamble	4	
shame	40	2a
shameful	11	5b
shameless	5	
shampoo	3	
shan't	5	
shape	62	1b
shapeless	9	
share	45	2a
shark	3	
sharp	49	2a
sharpen	16	4a
sharpener	3	
sharpness	4	
shatter	15	4b
shave	14	4b
shawl	7	
she	97	1a3
sheaf	9	
shear	16	4a
sheath	10	5b
sheaves	7	
Sheba	5	
shed	40	2a
sheen	5	
sheep	67	1b
sheer	5	
sheet	46	2a
shekel	5	
shelf	15	4b
shell	46	2a
shellac	3	
sheller	3	
shelter	39	2a
shelve	9	
shepherd	32	2b
shepherdess	3	
sheriff	9	
she's	5	
shew	7	
shield	28	3a
shift	20	3b
shilling	7	
Shiloh	4	
shin	6	
shine	64	1b

shingle	6		shrub	18	4a
ship	87	1a4	shrug	5	
shipment	12	5a	shrunk	5	
shipwreck	7		shudder	9	
shirt	30	2b	shun	19	3b
shiver	20	3b	shut	51	1b
shoal	4		shutter	8	
shock	33	2b	shuttle	3	
shod	5		shy	14	4b
shoe	72	1b	Siberia (n)	4	
shoemaker	18	4a	Sicily	4	
shone	25	3a	sick	60	1b
shook	36	2b	sicken	8	
shoot	39	2a	sickle	9	
shooter	4		sickly	8	
shop	50	1b	sickness	24	3a
shore	63	1b	side	131	1a2
shorn	6		sideboard	6	
short	94	1a4	sidelong	3	
shortage	3		sidewalk	16	4a
shorten	8		siege	11	5b
shot	40	2a	sieve	9	
shotgun	3		sift	14	4b
should	130	1a2	sigh	41	2a
shoulder	55	1b	sight	77	1a5
shouldst	6		sign	57	1b
shout	52	1b	signal	18	4a
shove	13	5a	signature	11	5b
shovel	15	4b	signet	6	
show	123	1a2	significant	4	
shower	36	2b	signify	10	5b
shrank	5		silence	42	2a
shred	5		silent	44	2a
shrewd	12	5a	silk	62	1b
shriek	19	3b	silken	9	
shrill	18	4a	silkworm	3	
shrine	15	4b	sill	7	
shrink	13	5a	silly	17	4a
shrivel	4		silver	80	1a5
shroud	11	5b	silverware	5	

silvery	8			six	91	1a4
similar	21	3b		sixpence	6	
similarity	3			sixteen	19	3b
similitude	4			sixteenth	5	
simmer	4			sixth	29	2b
Simon	12	5a		sixty	25	3a
simple	58	1b		size	69	1b
simplicity	14	4b		skate	20	3b
Simpson	5			skein	5	
simultaneous	3			skeleton	6	
sin	36	2b		sketch	10	5b
Sinai	4			skies	3	
since	108	1a3		skilful	17	4a
sincere	23	3a		skill	27	3a
sincerity	8			skim	14	4b
sinew	12	5a		skin	56	1b
sinewy	6			skip	20	3b
sinful	9			skirmish	6	
sing	80	1a5		skirt	37	2a
singe	4			skulk	4	
singer	16	4a		skull	12	5a
single	56	1b		sky	69	1b
singular	10	5b		skyscraper	3	
sink	42	2a		slab	8	
sinless	3			slack	9	
sinner	12	5a		slacken	6	
Sion	4			slain	21	3b
sip	11	5b		slam	7	
sir	69	1b		slander	10	5b
sire	20	3b		slanderous	3	
siren	6			slang	3	
sirloin	5			slant	14	4b
sirup	4			slap	9	
sis	3			slate	13	5a
sister	78	1a5		slaughter	15	4b
sisterhood	3			slave	39	2a
sit	85	1a4		slavery	13	5a
site	15	4b		slavish	4	
situate(d)	21	3b		slay	14	4b
situation	18	4a		slayer	4	

sled	11	5b	smelt	8	
sledge	12	5a	smile	58	1b
sleek	9		smite	15	4b
sleep	92	1a4	smith (S)	28	3a
sleeper	6		smithy	4	
sleepy	21	3b	smitten	9	
sleet	8		smock	7	
sleeve	20	3b	smoke	53	1b
sleeveless	3		smoker	5	
sleigh	13	5a	smooth	48	2a
slender	22	3b	smoothness	3	
slept	28	3a	smote	15	4b
slew	12	5a	smother	6	
slice	14	4b	snail	10	5b
slid	5		snake	19	3b
slide	28	3a	snap	28	3a
slight	41	2a	snare	15	4b
slim	4		snarl	9	
slime	6		snatch	19	3b
sling	11	5b	sneak	6	
slip	46	2a	sneer	7	
slipper	22	3b	sneeze	7	
slippery	16	4a	sniff	4	
slop	3		snip	5	
slope	29	2b	snore	8	
sloth	5		snort	7	
slothful	4		snout	7	
slow	70	1b	snow	72	1b
slug	8		snowball	3	
sluggard	4		snowdrop	3	
sluggish	3		snowflake	6	
slumber	28	3a	snowy	9	
slunk	4		snuff	13	5a
sly	17	4a	snuffle	3	
smack	9		snug	14	4b
small	118	1a2	so	188	1a1
smart	25	3a	soak	11	5b
smash	5		soap	26	3a
smear	5		soar	12	5a
smell	41	2a	sob	13	5a

sober	23	3a		sometime	83	1a5
sociable	3			somewhat	33	2b
social	22	3b		somewhere	19	3b
socialist	4			son	82	1a5
society	34	2b		song	68	1b
sock	10	5b		songster	5	
socket	8			sonnet	7	
sod	12	5a		soon	130	1a2
soda	9			soot	5	
sodden	4			sooth	8	
soever	7			soothe	11	5b
sofa	11	5b		soothsayer	4	
soft	79	1a5		sorcerer	6	
soften	16	4a		sorcery	6	
soil	58	1b		sordid	5	
sojourn	10	5b		sore	30	2b
sojourner	5			soreness	3	
solace	10	5b		sorrow	42	2a
sold	57	1b		sorrowful	11	5b
solder	4			sorry	42	2a
soldier	77	1a5		sort	54	1b
sole	35	2b		sought	30	2b
solemn	28	3a		soul	56	1b
solemnity	7			sound	87	1a4
solemnize	3			sounder	3	
solicit	12	5a		soup	25	3a
solid	24	3a		sour	15	4b
solidify	3			source	28	3a
solitary	18	4a		south	77	1a5
solitude	16	4a		southeast	7	
Solomon	11	5a		southeastern	5	
solution	10	5b		southern	34	2b
solve	20	3b		southward	11	5b
solvent	3			southwest	12	5a
somber (re)	6			southwestern	6	
some	181	1a1		sovereign	15	4b
somebody	25	3a		sovereignty	7	
somehow	6			sow	29	2b
someone	21	3b		space	50	1b
something	86	1a4		spacious	13	5a

spade	21	3b	sphere	20	3b
Spain	32	2b	spice	20	3b
spake	20	3b	spick	3	
span	13	5a	spicy	3	
spangle	13	5a	spider	17	4a
Spaniard	16	4a	spike	4	
spaniel	4		spill	11	5b
Spanish	37	2a	spilt	3	
spank	13	5a	spin	24	3a
spare	42	2a	spinach	5	
spark	20	3b	spinal	6	
sparkle	24	3a	spindle	11	5b
sparrow	26	3a	spine	5	
Sparta	4		spiral	3	
spat	5		spire	16	4a
speak	87	1a4	spirit	69	1b
speaker	20	3b	spiritual	14	4b
spear	26	3a	spit	15	4b
special	41	2a	spite	38	2a
specialist	3		spittoon	3	
specialty	3		splash	11	5b
species	4		spleen	8	
specify	3		splendid	37	2a
specimen	9		splendor	16	4a
specious	5		splinter	7	
speck	8		split	21	3b
speckle	11	5b	spoil	42	2a
spectacle	17	4a	spoiler	4	
spectator	6		spoke	52	1b
specter (re)	7		spoken	17	4a
speculation	4		spokesman	3	
sped	13	5a	sponge	12	5a
speech	45	2a	spontaneous	4	
speechless	6		spool	7	
speed	37	2a	spoon	34	2b
speedometer	3		sport	38	2a
speedy	15	4b	sportive	4	
spell	33	2b	sportsman	4	
spend	60	1b	spot	62	1b
spent	40	2a	spotless	4	

spouse	12	5a		stag	10	5b
spout	8			stage	28	3a
sprang	28	3a		stagger	17	4a
sprawl	4			staid	6	
spray	21	3b		stain	23	3a
spread	67	1b		stair	40	2a
spreader	4			staircase	3	
spree	6			stairway	4	
sprig	6			stake	22	3b
sprightly	8			stale	14	4b
spring	100	1a3		stalk	17	4a
springtime	9			stall	21	3b
sprinkle	22	3b		stammer	10	5b
sprite	9			stamp	40	2a
sprout	9			stand	118	1a2
spruce	4			standard	29	2b
sprung	18	4a		Stanley	12	5a
spry	3			stanza	3	
spun	13	5a		staple	7	
spur	17	4a		star	72	1b
spurn	11	5b		starch	4	
spy	30	2b		stare	21	3b
sq.	10	5b		stark	4	
squad	5			starlight	3	
squadron	8			starry	7	
squall	5			start	78	1a5
square	64	1b		startle	14	4b
squash	6			starvation	5	
squat	3			starve	26	3a
squaw	3			state	107	1a3
squeak	12	5a		stately	17	4a
squeeze	13	5a		statement	16	4a
squeezer	3			statesman	20	3b
squire	18	4a		station	56	1b
squirrel	26	3a		stationary	6	
St.	28	3a		stationery	6	
stab	12	5a		statistics	3	
stable	32	2b		statue	28	3a
stack	8			stature	12	5a
staff	21	3b		statute	8	

Stave to Straw

stave	9		stir	43	2a
stay	84	1a5	stirrup	9	
stead	12	5a	stitch	18	4a
steadfast	11	5b	St. Louis	4	
steadily	6		stock	51	1b
steady	23	3a	stocking(s)	31	2b
steak	11	5b	stole	28	3a
steal	41	2a	stolen	16	4a
stealth	6		stomach	18	4a
stealthy	3		stone	82	1a5
steam	43	2a	stony	13	5a
steamboat	9		stood	69	1b
steamer	20	3b	stool	17	4a
steamship	8		stoop	28	3a
steed	16	4a	stop	95	1a3
steel	45	2a	storage	7	
steep	36	2b	store	71	1b
steeple	14	4b	storehouse	6	
steer	23	3b	storekeeper	5	
stem	27	3a	stork	11	5b
stench	3		storm	63	1b
step	80	1a5	stormy	25	3a
Stephen	12	5a	story	84	1a5
stepmother	4		stout	25	3a
sterile	4		stove	28	3a
sterling	5		straggle	3	
stern	27	3a	straight	68	1b
Stevenson	4		straighten	8	
stew	7		straightway	10	5b
steward	6		strain	26	3a
Stewart	4		strainer	5	
stick	68	1b	strait	19	3b
stiff	29	2b	straiten	4	
stiffen	5		strand	13	5a
stifle	8		strange	66	1b
stile	6		stranger	34	2b
still	114	1a2	strangle	8	
stillness	12	5a	strap	15	4b
sting	23	3a	stratagem	5	
stink	7		straw	42	2a

strawberry	19	3b	stud	4	
stray	21	3b	Studebaker	4	
streak	10	5b	student	30	2b
stream	55	1b	studied (ies)	7	
streamer	3		studio	3	
street	91	1a4	studious	8	
strength	54	1b	study	68	1b
strengthen	14	4b	stuff	33	2b
strenuous	7		stumble	15	4b
stress	3		stumblingblock	4	
stretch	49	2a	stump	24	3a
stretcher	5		stun	5	
strew	10	5b	stung	9	
strewn	3		stunt	5	
stricken	12	5a	stupendous	4	
strict	19	3b	stupid	14	4b
stride	14	4b	stupidity	3	
strife	21	3b	sturdy	10	5b
strike	63	1b	sty	3	
string	35	2b	style	39	2a
strip	40	2a	stylish	5	
stripe	18	4a	subdue	20	3b
stripling	5		subject	54	1b
strive	20	3b	subjection	6	
strode	6		subjunctive	5	
stroke	36	2b	sublime	13	5a
stroll	10	5b	submission	6	
strong	98	1a3	submissive	4	
stronghold	3		submit	26	3a
strop	3		subscribe	5	
strove	11	5b	subscriber	6	
struck	34	2b	subscription	7	
structure	7		subsequent	8	
struggle	37	2a	subside	5	
strung	4		subsist	6	
strut	10	5b	substance	20	3b
stubble	7		substantial	14	4b
stubborn	16	4a	substantive	4	
stucco	3		substitute	16	4a
stuck	19	3b	subterranean	3	

subtle	11	5b	sultan	6	
subtract	8		sultry	5	
subtraction	3		sum	45	2a
suburb	11	5b	summary	3	
suburban	6		summer	87	1a4
subvert	4		summit	12	5a
subway	4		summon	23	3a
succeed	42	2a	sumptuous	9	
success	39	2a	sun	94	1a4
successful	25	3a	sunbeam	15	4b
succession	10	5b	sunburn	3	
successive	10	5b	Sunday	49	2a
successor	8		sunder	8	
succor	7		sundown	3	
such	157	1a1	sundry	4	
suck	15	4b	sunflower	5	
suckle	6		sung	22	3b
sudden	59	1b	sunk	17	4a
sue (S)	8		sunken	3	
Suez	3		sunless	4	
suffer	58	1b	sunlight	14	4b
sufferance	7		sunny	21	3b
sufferer	4		sunrise	11	5b
suffice	21	3b	sunset	20	3b
sufficiency	3		sunshine	34	2b
sufficient	27	3a	sup	9	
Suffolk	4		superb	5	
suffrage	6		superficial	3	
sugar	55	1b	superfluity	4	
suggest	24	3a	superfluous	9	
suggestion	9		superintendent	10	5b
suggestive	4		superior	31	2b
suit	67	1b	superiority	3	
suitable	14	4b	superlative	4	
suite	5		superstition	12	5a
suitor	8		superstitious	7	
sulky	4		supervision	4	
sullen	17	4a	supervisor	5	
sully	4		supper	46	2a
sulphur	8		supplant	6	

supple	4	
suppliant	5	
supplicate	5	
supplication	6	
supply	54	1b
support	40	2a
supporter	6	
suppose	65	1b
supposition	3	
suppress	10	5b
supremacy	3	
supreme	17	4a
sure	94	1a3
surety	6	
surf	3	
surface	36	2b
surfeit	5	
surge	10	5b
surgeon	7	
surgery	4	
surly	5	
surmise	6	
surmount	6	
surname	7	
surpass	12	5a
surplus	6	
surprise	56	1b
surrender	18	4a
surrey (S)	5	
surround	27	3a
survey	16	4a
surveyor	3	
survive	12	5a
survivor	6	
Susan	7	
suspect	18	4a
suspend	13	5a
suspender	4	
suspense	4	
suspicion	10	5b
suspicious	8	
sustain	17	4a
sustenance	3	
swain	12	5a
swallow	38	2a
swam	9	
swamp	16	4a
swan	19	3b
sware	5	
swarm	22	3b
swarthy	5	
sway	26	3a
swear	22	3b
sweat	17	4a
sweater	10	5b
Sweden	5	
Swedish	5	
sweep	36	2b
sweeper	6	
sweet	85	1a4
sweeten	7	
sweetheart	8	
sweetness	15	4b
swell	34	2b
swept	21	3b
swerve	7	
swift	45	2a
swiftness	4	
swim	46	2a
swimmer	3	
swine	12	5a
swing	36	2b
Swiss	12	5a
switch	10	5b
Switzerland	9	
swollen	8	
swoon	8	
sword	44	2a
swore	10	5b
sworn	15	4b

swum	3	
swung	5	
sycamore	6	
syllable	12	5a
sylph	4	
sylvan	6	
symbol	14	4b
symmetrical	5	
symmetry	3	
sympathetic	4	
sympathize	7	
sympathy	20	3b
symphony	3	
symptom	4	
synagogue	4	
syndicate	3	
Syracuse	4	
Syria	10	5b
syrup	8	
system	41	2a
tabby	4	
tabernacle (T)	9	
table	90	1a4
tablecloth	4	
tablespoon	4	
tablespoonful	5	
tablet	15	4b
tableware	3	
tabor	7	
tack	9	
tackle	7	
tact	6	
tadpole	5	
taffeta	5	
Taft	4	
tag	9	
tail	54	1b
tailor	31	2b
taint	9	

take	162	1a1
talcum	5	
tale	39	2a
talent	18	4a
talk	92	1a4
talker	7	
tall	56	1b
tallow	5	
tame	28	3a
tam-o'-shanter (T)	4	
tan	13	5a
tangle	6	
tank	15	4b
tanner	3	
tap	28	3a
tape	9	
taper	14	4b
tapestry	8	
tar	14	4b
tardy	15	4b
tare	4	
target	4	
tariff	7	
tarnish	3	
tarry	12	5a
Tarrytown	4	
Tarsus	4	
tart	9	
tartar (T)	4	
task	36	2b
tassel	10	5b
taste	53	1b
tatter	8	
tattoo	4	
taught	49	2a
taunt	4	
tavern	15	4b
tawny	5	
tax	40	2a
taxation	7	

taken 11 5b

taxicab	3			tenement	7	
Taylor	4			tenfold	3	
tea	46	2a		Tennessee	11	5b
teach	67	1b		tennis	9	
teacher	61	1b		tenor	9	
teakettle	3			tension	3	
team	31	2b		tent	48	2a
teapot	4			tenth	24	3a
tear	63	1b		term	39	2a
tease	10	5b		terminal	3	
teaspoon	8			terminate	5	
teat	5			termination	6	
tedious	12	5a		terrace	9	
teem	7			terrestrial	4	
teeth	33	2b		terrible	41	2a
telegram	14	4b		terrific	4	
telegraph	16	4a		terrify	9	
telephone	23	3a		territory	27	3a
telescope	6			terror	30	2b
tell	121	1a2		test	34	2b
teller	8			testament	7	
temper	23	3a		tester	4	
temperament	3			testify	11	5b
temperance	12	5a		testimony	14	4b
temperate	21	3b		tether	4	
temperature	21	3b		Texas	16	4a
tempest	17	4a		text	19	3b
tempestuous	8			textile	3	
temple	35	2b		texture	4	
temporal	5			Thames	9	
temporary	12	5a		than	157	1a1
tempt	26	3a		thank	83	1a5
temptation	14	4b		thankful	18	4a
tempter	5			thankfulness	6	
ten	90	1a4		thankless	5	
tenant	13	5a		thanksgiving (T)	21	3b
tend	27	3a		that	209	1a1
tendency	9			thatch	4	
tender	45	2a		that's	3	
tenderness	10	5b		thaw	11	5b

the	208	1a1	thin	55	1b
theater (re)	30	2b	thine	25	3a
theatrical	3		thing	157	1a1
thee	65	1b	think	124	1a2
theft	7		third	88	1a4
their	177	1a1	thirst	28	2b
them	181	1a1	thirsty	15	4b
theme	12	5a	thirteen	25	3a
themselves	58	1b	thirteenth	7	
then	173	1a1	thirtieth	6	
thence	25	3a	thirty	47	2a
thenceforth	6		this	191	1a1
theory	11	5b	thistle	14	4b
there	194	1a1	thither	16	4a
thereafter	6		tho	13	5a
thereby	16	4a	Thomas	26	3a
therefor	8		thorn	28	2b
therefore	57	1b	thorny	6	
therein	10	5b	thorough	33	2b
thereof	19	3b	thoroughfare	3	
thereon	14	4b	those	107	1a3
there's	13	5a	thou	58	1b
thereto	6		though	90	1a4
thereupon	16	4a	thought	96	1a3
therewith	7		thoughtful	12	5a
thermometer	10	5b	thoughtless	8	
these	142	1a2	thousand	94	1a4
they	194	1a1	thrall	7	
they'll	8		thrash	12	5a
they're	5		thread	49	2a
they've	3		threat	12	5a
thick	63	1b	threaten	30	2b
thicken	7		three	136	1a2
thicket	15	4b	threefold	4	
thickness	14	4b	threescore	7	
thief	28	3a	thresh (*see* thrash)		
thieve (s)	12	5a	threshold	11	5b
thievish	4		threw	37	2a
thigh	18	4a	thrice	18	4a
thimble	9		thrift	5	

thriftless	3			timber	18	4a
thrifty	8			timbrel	4	
thrill	17	4a		time	183	1a1
thrive	18	4a		timely	6	
thro'	13	5a		timid	16	4a
throat	35	2b		timorous	4	
throb	5			timothy (T)	10	5b
throne	35	2b		tin	25	3a
throng	21	3b		tincture	3	
throttle	3			tinder	5	
through	149	1a2		tinge	4	
throughout	32	2b		tingle	5	
throw	69	1b		tinker	3	
thrush	8			tinkle	11	5b
thrust	25	3a		tinsel	4	
thumb	20	3b		tint	8	
thump	12	5a		tiny	36	2b
thunder	34	2b		tip	39	2a
thunderbolt	8			tiptoe	3	
thunderstorm	3			tire (*noun*)	8	
Thursday	35	2b		tire (*verb*)	61	1b
thus	71	1b		tiresome	8	
thwart	8			'tis	23	3a
thy	48	2a		tissue	5	
thyself	20	3b		tit	7	
Tiber	5			tithe	5	
tick	22	3b		title	37	2a
ticket	23	3a		to	208	1a1
tickle	12	5a		toad	12	5a
tide	29	2b		toadstool	6	
tidings	13	5a		toast	14	4b
tidy	4			tobacco	25	3a
tie	50	1b		toboggan	4	
tiger	16	4a		tock	9	
tight	31	2b		today	80	1a5
tighten	4			toe	23	3a
tile	17	4a		together	97	1a3
till	78	1a5		toil	35	2b
tilt	9			toilet	10	5b
Tim	7			token	15	4b

told	75	1b	tortoise	12	5a
tolerable	5		torture	17	4a
tolerant	3		Tory	5	
tolerate	3		toss	29	2b
toleration	5		total	37	2a
toll	7		totter	9	
Tom	28	2b	touch	72	1b
tomahawk	4		tough	9	
tomato	12	5a	tour	7	
tomb	19	3b	tourist	5	
tombstone	5		tournament	4	
Tommy	13	5a	tow	10	5b
tomorrow	61	1b	toward(s)	75	1b
ton	25	3a	towel	14	4b
tone	29	2b	tower	42	2a
tongs	12	5a	town	93	1a4
tongue	55	1b	township	6	
tonic	5		toy	42	2a
tonight	36	2b	trace	36	2a
tonnage	9		track	36	2a
too	119	1a2	tract	16	4a
took	79	1a5	trade	55	1b
tool	29	2b	trader	12	5a
toot	5		tradesman	6	
tooth	29	2b	tradition	18	4a
toothache	4		traffic	16	4a
toothpick	6		tragedy	14	4b
top	90	1a4	tragic	7	
topic	10	5b	trail	23	3b
topmost	5		train	83	1a4
topple	5		traitor	17	4a
torch	14	4b	tramp	16	4a
tore	15	4b	trample	17	4a
torment	20	3b	trance	8	
tormentor	3		tranquil	9	
torn	25	3a	tranquillity	8	
torpedo	4		transact	4	
torpid	4		transaction	3	
torrent	13	5a	transcendent	4	
torrid	5		transfer	16	4a

transfigure	3			trespass	8	
transform	12	5a		trial	31	2b
transformer	3			triangle	9	
transgress	8			tribe	38	2a
transgression	6			tribulation	5	
transgressor	4			tribunal	6	
transient	8			tributary	17	4a
transit	6			tribute	18	4a
translate	15	4b		trick	33	2b
translation	4			trickle	6	
transmission	3			tricycle	3	
transmit	4			tried	49	2a
transparent	7			trifle	19	3b
transplant	4			trim	36	2a
transport	19	3b		trinity (T)	4	
transportation	14	4b		trip	68	1b
trap	29	2b		triple	5	
trash	5			triumph	23	3b
travail	5			triumphal	6	
travel	69	1b		triumphant	9	
traveler	40	2a		trivet	5	
traverse	10	5b		trivial	8	
tray	10	5b		trod	18	4a
treacherous	12	5a		trodden	4	
treachery	8			Trojan	4	
tread	30	2b		troll	10	5b
treason	15	4b		trolley	11	5b
treasure	37	2a		troop	29	2b
treasurer	9			trophy	10	5b
treasury	14	4b		tropic	8	
treat	47	2a		tropical	5	
treatment	19	3b		trot	23	3b
treaty	13	5a		troth	5	
treble	5			trouble	73	1b
tree	115	1a2		troublesome	8	
tremble	35	2a		trough	10	5b
tremendous	12	5a		trousers	18	4a
tremulous	6			trout	12	5a
trench	12	5a		trowel	3	
trend	5			troy (T)	8	

truant	8		turnip	11	5b
truce	3		turnpike	3	
truck	13	5a	turpentine	7	
trudge	8		turret	8	
true	95	1a3	turtle	14	4b
trump	6		tutor	11	5b
trumpet	25	3a	twain	9	
trundle	4		'twas	20	3b
trunk	42	2a	tweed	5	
truss	4		twelfth	14	4b
trust	56	1b	twelve	56	1b
trustee	4		twelvemonth	4	
trustworthy	4		twentieth	9	
trusty	9		twenty	73	1b
truth	67	1b	'twere	14	4b
truthful	5		twice	43	2a
try	95	1a3	twig	21	3b
tub	17	4a	twilight	19	3b
tube	16	4a	twill	4	
tuberculosis	3		'twill	15	4b
tuck	15	4b	twin	23	3a
Tues.	3		twine	16	4a
Tuesday	31	2b	twinkle	20	3b
tuft	9		twist	21	3b
tug	15	4b	twitch	5	
tulip	5		twitter	9	
tumble	26	3a	two	151	1a1
tumbler	5		twofold	5	
tumult	12	5a	'twould	4	
tumultuous	4		type	26	3a
tune	26	3a	typewriter	10	5b
tuneful	3		typewriting	3	
tunnel	11	5b	typical	5	
turban	6		tyrannical	3	
turbulent	7		tyrannous	3	
turf	13	5a	tyranny	15	4b
Turk	11	5b	tyrant	18	4a
turkey (T)	28	3a	Tyre	6	
Turkish	12	5a			
turn	124	1a2	udder	**5**	

ugly	29	2b		undergo	10	5b
ulster	3			underground	13	5a
ultimate	4			underline	5	
Ulysses	9			underneath	19	3b
umbrella	15	4b		undershirt	4	
umpire	4			understand	62	1b
unable	12	5a		understood	23	3a
unanimous	6			undertake	21	3b
unarm	7			undertaker	3	
unavoidable	3			undertook	6	
unaware	10	5b		underwaist	3	
unbearable	3			underwear	7	
unbelief	5			undeserved	3	
unbelieving	3			undisputed	4	
unborn	5			undisturbed	8	
unbound	8			undo	12	5a
unbroken	6			undone	9	
unceasing	3			undoubted	5	
uncertain	14	4b		undress	5	
uncertainty	3			undying	3	
unchanged	4			uneasy	12	5a
unchecked	3			unequal (ed)	8	
uncircumcised	4			unerring	4	
uncle	54	1b		uneven	9	
unclean	10	5b		unexpected	15	4b
uncleanness	3			unfavorable	4	
uncomfortable	11	5b		unfeeling	3	
uncommon	6			unfeigned	3	
unconcern	6			unfelt	3	
unconquerable	3			unfinished	5	
unconscious	16	4a		unfit	12	5a
uncouth	8			unfold	13	5a
uncover	12	5a		unfortunate	19	3b
uncut	3			unfriendly	5	
undaunted	5			unfruitful	5	
undecided	3			unfurl	5	
undefiled	4			unfurnished	3	
under	126	1a2		ungentle	5	
underbrush	4			ungodly	3	
underfoot	3			ungracious	3	

ungrateful	11	5b		unpleasant	10	5b
unguarded	6			unprofitable	6	
unhappy	31	2b		unpunished	4	
unhealthful	3			unreasonable	8	
unhealthy	4			unrestrained	3	
unheard	9			unrighteous	4	
unholy	3			unrighteousness	3	
unhurt	5			unruly	6	
uniform	25	3a		unsafe	6	
uniformity	3			unscrupulous	4	
uninjured	4			unseen	17	4a
unintelligible	3			unselfish	3	
union	42	2a		unsettled	8	
unique	3			unshaken	5	
unit	9			unsightly	4	
unite	70	1b		unskilful	4	
unity	11	5b		unsought	4	
universal	26	3a		unsound	3	
universe	9			unspeakable	8	
university	27	3a		unspotted	3	
unjust	20	3b		unstable	3	
unkind	11	5b		unstained	5	
unkindness	4			unsteady	4	
unknown	29	2b		unsuccessful	6	
unlawful	5			unsuspected	4	
unlearned	5			untaught	4	
unless	44	2a		unthinking	3	
unlettered	4			untidy	3	
unlike	14	4b		untie	8	
unload	6			until	108	1a3
unlock	10	5b		untimely	5	
unlooked	4			untiring	5	
unloose	3			unto	34	2b
unlucky	7			untold	5	
unmoved	6			untouched	3	
unnatural	6			untoward	4	
unnecessary	11	5b		untried	3	
unoccupied	7			untrod	5	
unpaid	4			untrue	7	
unpitied	4			unusual	17	4a

unveil	3			usual	55	1b
unweary (ied)	5			usurp	9	
unwelcome	8			usurpation	4	
unwieldy	3			usury	4	
unwilling	11	5b		Utah	4	
unwise	7			utensil	7	
unworthy	11	5b		utility	4	
up	186	1a1		utmost	17	4a
upbraid	8			utter	31	2b
upheld	6			utterance	13	5a
uphill	4			uttermost	7	
uphold	11	5b				
upholster	3			vacancy	8	
upholstery	3			vacant	20	3b
upland	5			vacate	3	
uplift	9			vacation	22	3b
upon	132	1a2		vacillate	4	
upper	41	2a		vacuum	3	
uppermost	4			vagabond	6	
upright	25	3a		vagrant	7	
uprightness	4			vague	8	
uprise	7			vail	6	
uproar	10	5b		vain	44	2a
uproot	7			vale	22	3b
upset	12	5a		valentine	9	
upside	5			valiant	14	4b
upstairs	10	5b		validity	3	
upward	25	3a		valley	60	1b
urchin	5			valor	13	5a
urge	32	2b		valuable	29	2b
urgent	9			value	57	1b
urn	15	4b		valve	8	
Uruguay	5			van	14	4b
us	134	1a2		vane	6	
U.S.	8			vanilla	4	
usage	4			vanish	25	3a
use	137	1a2		vanity	20	3b
useful	43	2a		vanquish	10	5b
useless	21	3b		vantage	6	
usher	6			vapor	25	3a

variable	4			verdict	5	
variation	3			verdure	5	
variegated	4			verge	10	5b
variety	25	3a		verify	6	
various	38	2a		verily	9	
varnish	9			vermin	3	
vary	26	3a		Vermont	6	
vase	8			vernal	4	
vassal	8			verse	27	3a
vast	33	2b		vertical	8	
vat	5			very	161	1a1
vault	16	4a		vesper	5	
vaunt	6			vessel	49	2a
veal	5			vest	23	3a
vegetable	30	2b		vestal	4	
vegetation	7			vesture	4	
vehement	6			veteran	9	
vehicle	6			veto	3	
veil	21	3b		vex	23	3a
vein	27	3a		vexation	10	5b
velvet	25	3a		via	5	
veneer	3			vial	5	
venerable	6			vibrate	6	
Venetian	4			vicar	5	
Venezuela	5			vice	26	3a
vengeance	17	4a		vicinity	10	5b
Venice	8			vicious	11	5b
venison	7			victim	17	4a
venom	6			victor	17	4a
venomous	4			victorious	18	4a
vent	9			victory	29	2b
ventilate	4			victual	7	
venture	22	3b		Vienna	7	
venturous	4			view	58	1b
Venus	7			viewless	4	
Vera Cruz	4			vigilance	4	
veranda	3			vigilant	4	
verb	8			vigor	20	3b
verbal	3			vigorous	9	
verdant	4			vile	17	4a

villa	5	
village	50	1b
villager	6	
villain	12	5a
villainous	4	
villainy	6	
vine	31	2b
vinegar	13	5a
vineyard	10	5b
vintage	5	
violate	15	4b
violation	4	
violence	20	3b
violent	19	3b
violet (V)	26	3a
violin	12	5a
viper	7	
virgin	22	3b
Virginia (n)	25	3a
virginity	5	
virtual	4	
virtue	33	2b
visage	8	
vise	3	
visible	14	4b
vision	22	3b
visionary	4	
visit	81	1a5
visitation	9	
visitor	18	4a
vital	10	5b
vivid	10	5b
vocabulary	7	
vocal	10	5b
voice	84	1a5
void	18	4a
voile	6	
volcano	7	
volley	5	
volt	4	

volume	28	2b
voluntary	10	5b
volunteer	7	
voluptuous	4	
vomit	6	
vote	34	2b
voter	8	
vouch	4	
vouchsafe	9	
vow	25	3a
vowel	7	
voyage	27	3a
vulgar	10	5b
vulture	5	
wade	9	
wafer	6	
waft	9	
wag	15	4b
wage	33	2b
wager	5	
wagon	38	2a
wagoner	6	
wail	17	4a
waist	33	2b
waistcoat	4	
wait	78	1a5
waiter	7	
wake	48	2a
wakeful	5	
waken	14	4b
Wales	8	
walk	108	1a3
walker (W)	6	
wall	97	1a3
wallet	7	
wallow	6	
walnut	11	5b
Walter	19	3b
Waltham	5	

virtuous 16 4a

wampum	6		watermelon	3	
wan	10	5b	waterproof	5	
wand	20	3b	watery	10	5b
wander	42	2a	watt	5	
wanderer	5		wave	62	1b
wane	7		waver	16	4a
want	110	1a3	wax	23	3a
wanton	15	4b	waxen	6	
wantonness	5		way	167	1a1
war	87	1a4	wayside	7	
warble	12	5a	wayward	7	
ward (W)	19	3b	we	170	1a1
wardrobe	8		weak	58	1b
ware	17	4a	weaken	8	
warehouse	6		weakness	26	3a
warfare	10	5b	weal	5	
warlike	8		wealth	43	2a
warm	88	1a4	wealthy	19	3b
warmth	15	4b	wean	5	
warn	34	2b	weapon	27	3a
warp	11	5b	wear	75	1b
warrant	17	4a	wearer	5	
warrior	27	3a	weariness	10	5b
warship	4		wearisome	4	
was	188	1a1	weary	29	2b
wash	72	1b	weasel	4	
washboard	5		weather	60	1b
washer	5		weathercock	7	
Washington	37	2a	weave	25	3a
wasn't	12	5a	weaver	9	
wasp	8		web	21	3b
wast	16	4a	wed	19	3b
waste	54	1b	we'd	3	
wasteful	3		wedding	14	4b
watch	84	1a5	wedge	13	5a
watchful	14	4b	wedlock	5	
watchman	10	5b	Wednesday	33	2b
watchword	3		wee	25	3a
water	139	1a2	weed	35	2b
waterfall	12	5a	weedy	4	

week	84	1a5		whenever	33	2b
weekly	10	5b		where	166	1a1
weep	38	2a		whereas	6	
weigh	43	2a		whereat	13	5a
weight	56	1b		whereby	14	4b
weighty	4			wherefore	17	4a
weird	5			wherein	18	4a
welcome	41	2a		whereof	10	5b
weld	6			whereon	10	5b
welfare	17	4a		wheresoever	6	
well	160	1a1		whereto	4	
we'll	19	3b		whereupon	7	
welt	4			wherever	24	3a
wench	7			wherewith	7	
wend	5			whether	59	1b
went	94	1a4		whew	6	
wept	21	3b		which	181	1a1
were	180	1a1		whichever	5	
we're	5			Whig	4	
wert	16	4a		while	138	1a2
west	72	1b		whilst	7	
western	39	2a		whim	4	
Westminster	5			whine	7	
westward	16	4a		whip	32	2b
wet	43	2a		whirl	22	3b
we've	7			whirlpool	4	
whale	8			whirlwind	13	5a
wharf	6			whisk	9	
wharves	7			whisker	6	
what	188	1a1		whisper	42	2a
whate'er	13	5a		whistle	39	2a
whatever	39	2a		whit	7	
whatsoever	19	3b		white (W)	120	1a2
wheat	52	1b		whiten	7	
wheel	53	1b		whiteness	4	
wheelbarrow	6			whitewash	4	
whelp	5			whither	21	3b
when	193	1a1		Whittington	6	
whence	32	2b		whiz	4	
whene'er	14	4b		who	184	1a1

[123]

whoever	16	4a	window	84	1a5
whole	97	1a3	Windsor	7	
wholesale	7		windy	9	
wholesome	16	4a	wine	47	2a
wholly	14	4b	wing	56	1b
whom	74	1b	wink	21	3b
whoop	7		winner	8	
whore	7		winter	91	1a4
whose	72	1b	wintry	9	
whosesoever	4		wipe	29	2b
whoso	6		wire	33	2b
why	143	1a2	wireless	9	
wick	4		Wisconsin	11	5b
wicked	31	2b	wisdom	36	2a
wickedness	12	5a	wise	64	1b
wide	89	1a4	wish	104	1a3
widen	6		wisp	4	
widow	23	3b	wist	4	
width	27	3a	wistful	5	
wield	9		wit	39	2a
wife	71	1b	witch	24	3a
wig	13	5a	witchcraft	7	
wight	8		with	208	1a1
wigwam	14	4b	withal	12	5a
wild	69	1b	withdraw	25	3a
wilderness	26	3a	withdrew	11	5b
wile	5		wither	19	3b
wilful	8		withheld	7	
will (W)	166	1a1	withhold	8	
William	46	2a	within	67	1b
willing	34	2b	without	107	1a3
willow	23	3b	withstand	13	5a
Willy	10	5b	withstood	6	
Wilson	8		witness	31	2b
wilt	16	4a	witty	11	5b
wily	4		wives	19	3b
win	58	1b	wizard	12	5a
Winchester	5		wk.	5	
wind	89	1a4	woe	24	3a
windmill	15	4b	woeful	9	

woke	16	4a		worry	20	3b
wolf	41	2a		worse	46	2a
wolves	11	5b		worship	27	3a
woman	120	1a2		worshipper	6	
womanhood	4			worst	33	2b
womankind	4			worsted	3	
womb	10	5b		worth	70	1b
women	44	2a		worthily	3	
won	40	2a		worthless	18	4a
wonder	64	1b		worthy	36	2a
wonderful	58	1b		wot	7	
wondrous	18	4a		would	166	1a1
wont	19	3b		wouldn't	15	4b
won't	29	2b		wouldst	8	
woo	18	4a		wound	44	2a
wood	92	1a4		wove	11	5b
woodbine	8			woven	14	4b
woodchuck	4			wrangle	4	
woodcutter	4			wrap	30	2b
wooden	29	2b		wrapper	5	
woodland	15	4b		wrath	21	3b
woodman	10	5b		wrathful	6	
woodpecker	9			wreath	27	3a
woodwork	3			wreathe	9	
woody	5			wreck	26	3a
woof	3			wren	13	5a
wool	38	2a		wrench	13	5a
woolen	15	4b		wrest	7	
wooly	3			wrestle	9	
word	114	1a2		wretch	16	4a
wore	28	2b		wretched	22	3b
work	151	1a1		wretchedness	6	
worker	22	3b		wriggle	3	
workman (men)	17	4a		wring	11	5b
workmanship	8			wringer	3	
workshop	5			wrinkle	18	4a
world	121	1a2		wrist	9	
worldly	12	5a		writ	14	4b
worm	32	2b		write	93	1a4
worn	31	2b		writer	23	3b

writhe	5		yoke	21	3b
written	43	2a	yolk	4	
wrong	63	1b	yon	17	4a
wrote	32	2b	yond	3	
wroth	9		yonder	28	2b
wrought	26	3a	yore	6	
wrung	5		York	8	
Wyoming	4		you	188	1a1
			you'd	11	5b
Xmas	6		you'll	18	4a
			young	97	1a3
yacht	3		youngster	3	
yard	58	1b	your	159	1a1
yarn	11	5b	you're	14	4b
yawn	14	4b	yours	22	3b
yd.	12	5a	yourself	49	2a
ye	32	2b	youth	49	2a
yea	20	3b	youthful	16	4a
year	151	1a1	you've	7	
yearly	11	5b	yr. (yrs.)	5	
yearn	12	5a			
yeast	7		zeal	20	3b
yell	17	4a	zealous	11	5b
yellow	50	1b	zephyr	6	
yeoman	4		zero	13	5a
yes	75	1b	zest	3	
yesterday	55	1b	zigzag	8	
yesternight	4		zinc	7	
yet	96	1a3	Zion	7	
yew	9		zone	26	3a
yield	47	2a	zoölogical	8	

a	burn	fall	here	mean
about	but	family	high	measure
above	buy	far	hill	meet
across	by	fast	him	men
add	call	father	himself	might
after	came	fear	his	mile
again	can	feel	hold	milk
against	care	feet	home	mind
air	carry	few	hope	mine
all	case	field	horse	miss
almost	cause	fill	hot	money
alone	certain	find	hour	month
along	change	fine	house	more
also	child	fire	how	morning
always	children	first	hundred	most
am	church	five	I	mother
among	city	floor	if	mountain
an	clear	flower	in	move
and	close	fly	into	much
another	cold	follow	is	must
answer	color	food	it	my
any	come	foot	its	name
apple	company	for	just	near
are	corn	form	keep	need
arm	could	found	kill	never
around	country	four	kind	new
as	course	free	king	next
ask	cover	fresh	know	night
at	cross	friend	known	no
away	cut	from	land	north
back	dark	front	large	not
bad	day	full	last	nothing
ball	dead	garden	late	now
bank	dear	gave	laugh	number
be	death	general	law	of
bear	deep	get	lay	off
beautiful	did	girl	lead	often
became	die	give	learn	old
because	do	given	leave	on
bed	does	glad	left	once
been	done	go	length	one
before	door	God	less	only
begin	down	gold	let	open
behind	draw	good	letter	or
being	dress	got	lie	order
believe	drink	great	life	other
best	drive	green	light	our
better	drop	ground	like	out
between	during	grow	line	over
big	each	had	little	own
bird	ear	hair	live	paper
black	early	half	long	part
blow	earth	hand	look	pass
blue	east	happy	lost	pay
body	eat	hard	love	people
book	egg	has	low	person
both	end	have	made	picture
box	enough	he	make	piece
boy	even	head	man	place
bread	ever	hear	many	plain
bring	every	heart	mark	plant
brother	eye	heavy	matter	play
brought	face	help	may	please
build	fair	her	me	point

[127]

poor	something	until
power	sometime	up
present	son	upon
pretty	soon	us
put	sound	use
quick	south	very
rain	speak	visit
raise	spring	voice
reach	stand	wait
read	start	walk
ready	state	wall
reason	stay	want
receive	step	war
red	still	warm
remain	stone	was
remember	stop	watch
rest	story	water
rich	street	way
ride	strong	we
right	such	week
river	summer	well
road	sun	went
rock	sure	were
roll	sweet	what
room	table	when
round	take	where
run	talk	which
said	tell	while
sail	ten	white
same	than	who
save	thank	whole
saw	that	why
say	the	wide
school	their	will
sea	them	wind
second	then	window
see	there	winter
seem	these	wish
seen	they	with
send	thing	without
sent	think	woman
serve	third	wood
set	this	word
several	those	work
shall	though	world
she	thought	would
ship	thousand	write
short	three	year
should	through	yet
show	till	you
side	time	young
sight	to	your
silver	today	
since	together	
sing	too	*End of*
sister	top	*first*
sit	town	*500*
six	train	
sleep	tree	
small	true	
so	try	
soft	turn	
soldier	two	
some	under	

[128]

able	car
account	careful
act	catch
afraid	cent
afternoon	center
age	chair
ago	chance
allow	charge
already	chief
although	choose
American	Christmas
amount	circle
animal	class
anything	clean
appear	clock
army	cloth
arrive	clothe (ing)
art	clothes
article	cloud
attend	coal
baby	coast
bag	coat
band	coming
basket	command
battle	common
bay	complete
beast	condition
beat	contain
beauty	continue
bee	cook
began	cool
bell	corner
belong	cost
beside	count
bill (B)	court
bit	cow
bless	cried
blind	crowd
blood	crown
board	cry
boat	cup
bone	dance
born	dare
bottom	date
bow	daughter
branch	deal
brave	decide
break	delight
breakfast	demand
bridge	desire
bright	destroy
broad	difference
broken	different
brook	dinner
brown	direct
building	discover
built	distance
business	divide
busy	doctor
butter	dog
cake	don't
cannot	double
cap	doubt
captain	dream

dry	gone	list	perfect	shop	thus
dust	government	listen	perhaps	shore	tie
duty	grace (G)	load	pick	shoulder	tire (d)
easy	grain	lord	plan	shout	told
edge	grant	lose	pleasant	shut	tomorrow
eight	grass	loss	pleasure	sick	tongue
either	grave	lot	possible	sign	took
else	gray	loud	post	silk	touch
enemy	grew	lower	pound	simple	toward (s)
England	guard	mail	practice	single	trade
English	guess	manner	prepare	sir	travel
enjoy	guide	march (M)	press	size	trip
enter	hall	market	price	skin	trouble
entire	hang	master	prince	sky	trust
equal	happen	meat	promise	slow	truth
escape	hat	member	proper	smile	twelve
evening	health	met	proud	smoke	twenty
everything	heard	middle	prove	snow	uncle
except	heat	mill	public	soil	understand
expect	heaven	minute	pull	sold	unite
express	height	moment	pure	song	usual
extend	held	moon	purpose	sort	valley
fact	herself	mount	quarter	soul	value
famous	hide	mouth	queen	space	view
fancy	history	Mr.	question	spend	village
farm	hole	Mrs.	quiet	spirit	wash
farmer	honor	music	quite	spoke	waste
fat	however	myself	race	spot	wave
favor	hunt	narrow	ran	spread	weak
feed	hurry	nation	rapid	square	wear
fell	hurt	natural	rather	star	weather
fellow	husband	nature	real	station	weight
felt	ice	necessary	reply	stick	west
fence	ill	neck	report	stock	wheat
fight	important	neighbor	require	stood	wheel
figure	inch	neither	ring	store	whether
finger	increase	nest	rise	storm	whom
finish	indeed	New York	roof	straight	whose
firm	Indian	nice	rose	strange	wife
fish	instead	nine	row	stream	wild
fit	interest	noise	rule	strength	win
fix	iron	none	rush	strike	wing
flow	island	noon	sad	study	wise
following	join	nor	safe	subject	within
force	journey	nose	salt	sudden	wonder
forest	joy	note	sand	suffer	wonderful
forget	judge	notice	sat	sugar	worth
former	jump	O	season	suit	wrong
forth	kept	oak	seat	supply	yard
forward	kiss	object	seed	suppose	yellow
fourth	knee	ocean	seek	surprise	yes
France	knew	offer	seize	tail	yesterday
French	labor	office	self	tall	
fruit	lady	officer	sell	taste	
gain	laid	oh	separate	teach	
game	lake	outside	service	teacher	*End of*
gate	least	page	settle	tear	*second*
gather	led	pain	seven	thee	*500*
gentle	leg	paint	shade	themselves	
gentleman	lesson	pair	shake	therefore	
gift	lie	party	shape	thick	
glass	lift	path	sheep	thin	
going	lion	peace	shine	thou	
golden	lip	pen	shoe	throw	

accept
according
action
address
admire
advance
advantage
afterward
agree
ah
aid
alive
America
ancient
angel
anger
angry
apart
apply
appoint
approach
April
asleep
attempt
August
aunt
awake
bake
bare
bark
barn
base
beam
became
beg
behold
below
bend
beneath
bid
bind
birth
bite
bitter
blame
block
blossom
boil
bold
border
bottle
bought
bound
bowl
breast
breath
breathe
brick
brush
burst
bury
bush
camp
card

carriage
cast
castle
cat
cattle
caught
chamber
character
Charles
charm
chase
check
cheek
cheer
chicken
choice
chose (n)
claim
climb
cock
coffee
college
comfort
companion
compare
connect
consent
consider
constant
content
copy
correct
cotton
cousin
cream
creature
creep
crop
cruel
curtain
custom
danger
darkness
dash
dawn
debt
December
declare
deed
degree
delay
deliver
depart
describe
desert
desk
diamond
difficult
direction
dish
distant
dollar
dozen
drew

drown
earn
effect
elect
employ
empty
ere
especial
establish
Europe
event
evil
exact
example
excellent
experience
explain
fail
faint
faith
faithful
fare
farther
fashion
fault
feast
feather
feeling
fierce
fifteen
fifty
final
finally
flag
flame
flash
flat
flesh
flour
fold
folk
fond
foreign
fortune
forty
fought
fox
frame
freedom
frequent
Friday
friendly
frost
fun
fur
furnish
further
future
gay
George
German
giant
glory
goat

goose
governor
grand
grape
greet
guest
gun
handle
hardly
harm
harry (H)
harvest
haste
hate
hay
heel
hen
hence
Henry
hollow
honest
honey
horn
huge
human
hung
hungry
idea
imagine
immediate
include
inside
intend
invite
issue
itself
jack (J)
James
July
June
justice
key
kindly
kingdom
kitchen
knife
knight
knock
knowledge
lack
lad
lamb
lamp
language
leader
lean
leap
leather
level
liberty
limit
lock
lodge
London

loose
lovely
lying
machine
mad
maid
main
map
marry
Mary
mass
match
material
meadow
meal
meant
melt
memory
mention
merchant
mere
message
midnight
mighty
million
mistake
mix
Monday
mouse
murmur
nail
native
net
news
noble (ly)
November
nurse
nut
obey
observe
obtain
occasion
occupy
o'clock
October
oil
opinion
orange
ought
owe
pack
paid
palace
parent
park
particular
peep
permit
pie
pig
pile
pin
pipe
pity

plate	servant	thread	absolute	candle
plenty	seventy	thy	accompany	candy
pocket	sew	tip	accomplish	can't
poet	shadow	title	acre	cave
pole	shame	total	actual	cease
port	share	tower	addition	celebrate
possess	sharp	toy	admit	central
pot	shed	trace	advice	century
potato	sheet	track	advise	cheap
pour	shell	traveler	Africa	cheerful
praise	shelter	treasure	aim	cheese
pray	shoot	treat	alarm	cherry
prayer	shot	tribe	alike	chest
prefer	sigh	tried	anxious	chimney
presence	silence	trim	appearance	china (C)
preserve	silent	trunk	approve	Christian
president	skirt	twice	arch	citizen
prevent	slave	union	arrange	clay
pride	slight	unless	arrow	clerk
print	slip	upper	ashamed	cloak
prisoner	smell	useful	Asia	club
private	smooth	vain	assist	coach
proceed	sorrow	various	assure	coin
produce	sorry	vessel	ate	collar
protect	Spanish	wagon	Atlantic	collect
provide	spare	wake	attack	colony
pupil	special	wander	attention	comfortable
purchase	speech	Washington	authority	commerce
push	speed	wealth	automobile	compass
quality	spent	weep	autumn	complain
quantity	spite	weight	avenue	concern
railroad	splendid	welcome	avoid	conduct
range	spoil	western	await	congress
rank	sport	wet	awful	conquer
rate	stair	whatever	ax (axe)	consist
record	stamp	whisper	balance	control
refuse	steal	whistle	beach	copper
regard	steam	William	bean	cottage
region	steel	wine	beard	council
regular	stir	wisdom	begun	couple
rejoice	straw	wit	belt	courage
remove	stretch	wolf	bench	crack
rent	strip	women	benefit	create
repair	struggle	won	bent	crew
repeat	style	wool	berry	crime
represent	succeed	worse	beyond	crow
respect	success	worthy	birthday	crush
result	sum	wound	blade	cure
roar	Sunday	written	blaze	curl
rod	supper	yield	blessing	current
Roman	support	yourself	bloom	curse
root	swallow	youth	boast	daily
rough	swift		boot	dangerous
royal	swim		bore	deceive
ruin	sword	*End of*	bosom	deck
satisfy	system	*third*	brass	defend
scale	tale	*500*	bride	deny
scarce	taught		brief	depend
scatter	tea		British	descend
search	tender		broke	deserve
secret	tent		brow	determine
secure	term		bud	devil
sense	terrible		button	dew
September	thirty		calm	Dick

dig	forgot	lace	period	scene	toil
dine	forgotten	ladies	Peter	score	Tom
disappear	fork	lap	pine	seal	tone
disease	fort	latter	pink	section	tonight
district	fountain	lawn	pluck	seldom	tool
divine	freeze	lazy	pond	select	tooth
doll	friendship	league	porch	serious	toss
dot	fright	library	portion	severe	trap
drag	frighten	limb	possession	shepherd	tread
drain	frozen	linen	preach	shirt	tremble
dread	furniture	log	precious	shock	trial
dreadful	garment	lover	principal	shook	trick
drill	gaze	lumber	prison	shower	troop
drove	gem	maiden	prize	sin	Tuesday
drum	generous	maintain	probable	sixth	ugly
duck	Germany	manage	product	slope	unhappy
dwell	glance	manufacture	profit	society	unknown
eager	globe	marble	prompt	sole	unto
eagle	glorious	married	pronounce	somewhat	urge
earnest	glove	mate	proof	sore	utter
ease	glow	medicine	property	sought	valuable
easily	goes	mercy	province	southern	vast
echo	govern	metal	punish	sow	vegetable
effort	gown	mild	purple	Spain	victory
eighteen	grade	minister	purse	spell	vine
elate	grandmother	mistress	pursue	spoon	virtue
eleven	grief	mock	quarrel	spy	volume
empire	grind	model	quit	stable	vote
engage	group	modern	rabbit	standard	wage
engine	grove	mortal	rail	steep	waist
entrance	gulf	motion	rare	stiff	warn
erect	hail	mourn	rat	stocking	weary
error	hammer	mud	ray	stranger	Wednesday
everybody	handkerchief	national	really	string	weed
examine	handsome	needle	rear	stroke	whence
exchange	happiness	neglect	recover	struck	whenever
excuse	harbor	newspaper	reign	student	whip
expense	hasten	nobody	render	stuff	wicked
extreme	heap	nod	request	sunshine	willing
fade	herd	northern	restore	superior	wipe
fairy	hero	oblige	retire	surface	wire
false	hid	occur	review	sweep	witness
fame	hire	odd	ribbon	swell	wont
familiar	hit	operation	ripe	swing	wooden
fan	holiday	opportunity	roast	tailor	wore
farewell	hook	opposite	rob	task	worm
fasten	host	orchard	robe	team	worn
fate	hunter	organ	Robert	teeth	worst
favorite	idle	owl	robin	temple	wrap
feature	I'll	owner	rode	terror	wrote
February	I'm	oxygen	Rome	test	yonder
fed	impossible	pace	rope	theater	ye
fetch	improve	pale	rub	thirst	
fever	indicate	pan	rude	thorn	
fleet	industry	pardon	sack	thorough	*End of*
flew	influence	partly	sacrifice	threaten	*fourth*
flight	inform	pasture	saddle	throat	*500*
float	instant	patient (ly)	safety	throne	
flock	joyful	pattern	sailor	throughout	
flood	judgment	pearl	saint	thunder	
foe	Kate	pencil	sake	Thursday	
foolish	kick	penny	sale	tide	
forbid	kid	per	sang	tight	
forehead	kindness	perform	Saturday	tiny	

absent	Columbus	eastern	howl	merit
accident	column	education	humble	messenger
accustom	combine	Edward	humor	method
acquaintance	compel	Egypt	hunger	midst
active	conceal	eighth	hush	military
affect	conclude	election	hut	mirror
agriculture	condemn	electric	image	mist
alas	confess	embrace	immortal	moderate
aloud	conscience	emperor	importance	modest
annual	continent	encourage	incline	monument
appeal	contract	endure	independent	moral
area	contrary	enormous	India	movement
arise	convenient	entertain	individual	multiply
armor	conversation	envy	information	murder
arose	cord	estate	injure	musical
ascend	costly	eternal	ink	mystery
aside	couch	eve (E)	innocent	naked
assembly	couldst	everywhere	inquire	navy
author	counsel	exceed	insect	neat
average	county	excite	instance	necessity
bade	credit	exclaim	instruct	negro
barrel	crime	factory	instruction	neighborhood
bath	cultivate	fearful	instrument	numerous
bathe	cunning	female	introduce	oat
beggar	curious	file	invitation	o'er
Billy	Dan	flatter	isle	offend
blacksmith	darling	fled	Italian	offense
blank	dart	flies	Italy	official
blew	decay	flutter	jar	olive
blush	decline	folly	jaw	oppose
bolt	deer	forgive	jewel	ordinary
bond	defense	foul	job	original
borrow	delicate	foundation	joint	ornament
bough	den	fowl	Joseph	otherwise
brain	department	frank (F)	kettle	ours
brake	depth	freight	kitten	ourselves
breeze	design	fret	knit	package
bubble	despair	frog	ladder	pail
bull	despise	fully	lame	palm
bunch	destruction	funeral	lane	pant
burden	develop	gas	lark	papa
bushel	devote	glitter	Latin	paradise
butcher	didn't	goodness	laughter	parcel
California	difficulty	gracious	lend	parlor
canal	dim	gradual	lest	passage
canst	dip	grandfather	lightning	passenger
cape	discovery	grateful	likely	passion
carpenter	display	grieve	lily	patch
cart	dispose	groan	lively	patience
carve	dispute	growth	local	Paul
cell	distinct	guilty	locate	pea
cellar	distress	ha	lone	peach
chapel	disturb	habit	luck	pear
charity	ditch	harness	luxury	peculiar
chill	division	heal	magic	perceive
chop	domestic	henceforth	magnificent	perish
circumstance	doth	hind	majority	Philip
civil	dove	hither	maker	physician
clap	draft	honorable	mamma	pillow
clasp	droop	hoof	mankind	pit
cliff	dull	hop	marriage	pitch
climate	dumb	hospital	mast	plot
coarse	Dutch	hotel	mayor	plow
colt	dying	household	mend	plum

plunge	scream	Thomas
poem	senate	thrust
poison	sentence	ticket
pony	settlement	tin
population	seventh	'tis
position	shalt	tobacco
powder	shield	toe
practical	shone	ton
prevail	sickness	torn
prey	sincere	trumpet
priest	sixty	tumble
princess	skill	tune
problem	slept	turkey (T)
process	slide	twin
proclaim	slumber	type
professor	smart	understood
progress	smith (S)	uniform
prophet	snap	universal
proportion	soap	university
propose	sober	upright
prospect	solid	upward
publish	somebody	vanish
puff	soup	vapor
pump	source	variety
punishment	sparkle	vary
rack	sparrow	vein
rag	spear	velvet
rage	spin	verse
raw	sprang	vest
realm	squirrel	vex
recent	St.	vice
recognize	stain	violet
reduce	starve	Virginia
register	statue	vow
relate	steady	voyage
relation	stem	warrior
relative	stern	wax
relief	sting	weakness
relieve	stole	weapon
religion	stoop	weave
religious	stormy	wee
representative	stout	wherever
reserve	stove	width
resolve	strain	wilderness
reveal	stump	witch
revenge	submit	withdraw
reward	successful	woe
rib	sufficient	worship
rice	suggest	wreath
rid	summon	wreck
ridge	surround	wrought
robber	sway	zone
robe	tame	
route	tap	
rubber	telephone	*End of*
rug	temper	*fifth*
ruler	tempt	*500*
Russia(n)	tend	
sacred	tenth	
salary	territory	
scare	thence	
science	thief	
scorn	thine	
scratch	thirteen	